MW00533403

The CIO
Playbook

The CIO Playbook

Strategies and Best Practices for IT Leaders to Deliver Value

Nicholas R. Colisto

WILEY

John Wiley & Sons, Inc.

Published by John Wiley & Sons, Inc., Hoboken, New Jersey.
Published simultaneously in Canada.

For general information on our other products and services or for technical support, please
contact our Customer Care Department within the United States at (800) 762-2974,
outside the United States at (317) 572-3993 or fax (317) 572-4002.

Wiley also publishes its books in a variety of electronic formats. Some content that appears
in print may not be available in electronic books. For more information about Wiley
products, visit our web site at www.wiley.com.

Library of Congress Cataloging-in-Publication Data:
Colisto, Nicholas R.,
    The CIO playbook : strategies and best practices for IT leaders to deliver value /
Nicholas R. Colisto.
        p. cm.
            ISBN 978-1-118-34759-1 (cloth); ISBN 978-1-118-38518-0 (ebk.);
            ISBN 978-1-118-41118-6 (ebk.); ISBN 978-1-118-41119-3 (ebk.)
1. Chief information officers. 2. Information technology–Management. 3. Information
resources management. I. Title.
HD30.2.C6245 2012
658.4'038–dc23

                                                                2012012392

Printed in the United States of America

10 9 8 7 6 5 4 3 2 1

For Joanne, Alexandra, and Evan

Contents

Preface

The only thing to do with good advice is to pass it on. It is never of any use to oneself.

—*Oscar Wilde*

These are times for transformation. The economy is shifting from recession to recovery. Companies are transitioning from cost containment to value creation. Chief information officers (CIOs) are uniquely positioned to help their organizations create a critical turning point by leveraging technology to drive innovation and business growth.

Whether you are an information technology (IT) leader or a business professional who leverages technology to help drive results, you will find that this book offers insightful and practical advice and strategies to help you maximize the effect of IT on your business. While the technologies constantly change at a dramatic pace, the practices I describe in this book are timeless and can help you transform your IT department from a mere order taker to a high-performance organization that delivers extraordinary business outcomes, despite this era of turbulent economic challenges.

To begin this journey, I examine the pressing questions that IT practitioners ask themselves and often struggle with answering: How do I truly partner with my business peers? How do I ensure that my team is focused on the right innovations? How do I deliver high-quality products and services that are embraced by my user community? What strategies should I employ to run my department like a business and measure performance? How can I manage and minimize risks so that my company can continue to operate effectively and protect its reputation—particularly in this era of social networking, mobilization, and cloud computing? How can I attract, motivate, and retain a talented team that is focused on the same vision?

In this book, I share a framework that I have developed over my career that includes practical strategies and tactics to address these questions and help IT leaders truly transform their organizations. The framework involves seven steps:

1. **Partner.** Establish strong relationships with internal and external stakeholders to create long-term competitive advantage.
2. **Organize.** Define the organizational structure and processes needed to run IT effectively and efficiently so that it delivers value-added products and services, seeks continual improvement, and is prepared to adapt to business change.
3. **Innovate.** Build cost-effective and high-performance technology products and services that deliver value and are strategically aligned with business goals and objectives.
4. **Deliver.** Implement products and services to improve bottom-line performance for your company.
5. **Support.** Provide superior services to maximize the return on investment in business technology.
6. **Protect.** Manage and minimize risks so that your company can continue to operate effectively and protect its reputation.
7. **Grow.** Attract, motivate, and retain a talented team that works toward a common vision and mission.

Each step involves a set of practices designed to help you achieve success. The steps are interrelated and complement one another as part of an overall effort to establish a high-performance IT organization.

I have dedicated a chapter to each of these steps and described the best practices. I realize that every organization is unique and my strategies and tactics may not always fit the circumstances due to cultural, political, and organizational constraints. That being said, I have had the pleasure of working for eight companies, spanning seven industries, and have yet to come across a situation where most, if not all, of these steps could not be applied. I have also enlisted the help of IT leaders and other executives from a diverse set of industries and practices to share their strategies and stories in this book.

I promise you, this book is not filled with theoretical concepts or prosaic monologues; rather, it provides a comprehensive set of proven strategies, tools, and techniques. It's tiring to read all of those books, blogs, and articles that lecture IT leaders on getting a seat at the executive table but never explain *how* to actually do it. It is also frustrating to read a book or attend a conference and not walk away with salient points of advice that you can readily apply. For that reason, I conclude each chapter with a list of tips that I refer to as my Top Plays.

Everyone learns differently: some like theory, others enjoy reading interviews with executives, and still others prefer to stumble along and learn from experience. Will Rogers once wrote, "There are three kinds of men, ones that learn by reading, a few who learn by observation, and the rest of them have to pee on the electric fence and find out for themselves."

In my experience, IT professionals generally appreciate structure and pragmatic advice. They have a predilection for methodology, process, policies, and templates. They want to face a chaotic world equipped with an orderly approach so they can enable their businesses to grow and prosper. I suppose that is why they entered the profession in the first place—it's part of their DNA. And with a field as dynamic and complex as IT, theory and entertaining anecdotes alone are not enough.

So for that reason, I decided to write this book: to create order from chaos and provide a comprehensive set of specific steps that IT leaders can take to deliver extraordinary results despite tumultuous times. Think of this book as the first how-to guide for creating a high-performance IT organization that delivers value-added products and services to employees, customers, and shareholders.

Leading an IT organization in an age when there is an unprecedented demand on technology to drive business growth requires CIOs to learn and apply these seven transformative steps. I want to arm leaders with the tools to get them started right away. For that reason, I have developed templates for each of the seven steps described in this book. The templates are straightforward and easily customizable by you or your staff to create similar documents for your own organization. They can be found on the companion website for this book (see the About the Website page for more information).

Acknowledgments

T his book is a compilation of my work experience as well as the result of research that I conducted. I would like to acknowledge the many people who have helped me along the way.

First, I offer my sincere gratitude to the executives who participated in the interviews: Gary Boyd, Jeff Boyd, Rich Brennen, David Colville, Michael Del Priore, Greg Fell, Jim Gery, Jon Harding, Ken Harris, John Hinkle, David Kaufman, Richard Lattmann, Brian R. Lurie, Diane Montalto, Ken Murdoch, Kevin Nash, and Phil Schneidermeyer. I hope that this book captures your excellent insights.

Next, I would like to thank the many managers and mentors I have had during my career: Daren Bien, Michael Clifford, Jeff Hoffman, Ara K. Hovnanian, Holger Huels, Tom Lesica, Joan Pertak, Joanne Raimondo, Ron Rose, and J. Larry Sorsby. I am grateful for your good advice, counsel, and support.

I would also like to acknowledge my IT staff at Hovnanian Enterprises Inc. and the many members of my staff whom I have had the pleasure to work with throughout my career. I thank you for your passion, commitment, and drive to be the best at what you do. Without you, this book would not have been possible.

Many thanks to Sanjog Aul, Cecilia Biegel, Jon Hernandez, Mike Keizur, Hunter Muller, Kate Rood, Bethany Simpson, and Avery Wright for inviting me to lecture at industry events and forums and encouraging me to write. You helped me find my voice for this book, and for that I am deeply grateful.

I would also like to thank Sheck Cho, Kimberly Monroe-Hill, and Stacey Rivera, my editors at John Wiley & Sons, who believed in me and gave me such wonderful guidance and advice.

A sincere thank-you to the people that have inspired me to be socially responsible by inviting me to participate on academic and health-care boards: Serena DiMaso, Esq.; Dr. David Finegold; David L. Flood; Elizabeth Milewski; Thomas Setaro; Dr. Deborah Silver; Wendell Smith, Esq.; and Aleta You. The only thing you take with you when you leave this earth is what you leave behind, and I am grateful for the opportunity to serve my community.

I want to acknowledge the support and love of my parents. You have always been so supportive and have encouraged me to chase my dreams. I love you so much.

And thanks to my sister, Linda, for her love and support that mean so much to me. She typed my first report in high school. I should have asked her to type this book for me. She types much faster than I do.

I have also been fortunate to have a father-in-law and a mother-in-law who have supported me and shared invaluable lessons in life and business that have always guided me and still do today. And thanks to all of my sisters-in-law and brothers-in-law and their families, who keep me grounded—as only a large Italian family can do—and are a constant reminder of what's most important.

Most of all, I thank my wife, Joanne, for her unconditional love and unwavering support as I hunkered down in my home office to write this book on many evenings and weekends. And I thank my children, Alexandra and Evan, for being so understanding, loving, and supportive.

Chapter 1

Step 1: Partner

If we are together nothing is impossible. If we are divided all will fail.
—Winston Churchill

Partner: Establish strong relationships with internal and external stakeholders to create long-term competitive advantage.

Your success greatly depends on your relationships with others. Whether you are trying to drive results within your team, with stakeholders across your company, or with suppliers, your ability to create positive business outcomes will rest on the strength of your business relationships. Partnerships begin with having a clear understanding of a company's vision, goals, and strategies. This chapter describes the stages of a business partnership and how to build an IT strategic plan, in cooperation with your team and business partners, so that everyone has a clear picture of the value IT will contribute to the company.

Partnership versus Alignment

Year after year, IT survey results inevitably state that one of the top priorities for the coming year will be to align IT with the business. The topic certainly gets a lot of attention and is often the source of many articles, postings, books, and presentations. Out of curiosity, I performed a search on Google, and it returned an astonishing 3.3 million results on the topic.

Why do so many CIOs struggle with alignment? Perhaps the answer is that they focus too much attention on aligning with the business rather than partnering with it. Are these just two different words with the same meaning, or is partnering in a different category altogether? Let's look at the definitions. *Alignment* is a state of agreement or cooperation. *Partnership*, however, is the state of being associates or colleagues. Partnership is about establishing strong relationships with internal and external stakeholders to create a long-term competitive advantage.

Given these definitions, alignment is being an order taker, while partnership is about people joining as colleagues in business—two very different relationships. Which relationship would you rather have with your fellow business leaders?

In successful partnerships, three common elements repeatedly and consistently emerge: impact, intimacy, and vision. *Impact* describes a partnership's capacity to deliver tangible results. Successful partnerships increase productivity, add value, and ultimately improve profitability. *Intimacy* is a challenging word; it conjures up images of people relating on an intensely close level. That's exactly what successful partners do in a business context. Successful partnerships also have *vision*: a compelling picture of what the partnership can achieve and, specifically, how it is going to get there.[1]

Build Business Partnerships

There are three stages of a business partnership: earning trust, setting priorities, and creating business strategy. If you achieve these stages, you will ascend from merely aligning with the business to being a valued business leader in your organization. Let's take a closer look at how it works.

Earning Trust

The first stage in building a partnership is earning trust. Relationships may be built, but trust is earned—and it's necessary for a true partnership. Once you have demonstrated that you can be relied on to deliver real value to the company, you become a trusted supplier of products and services. The more value you deliver, the more credible and respected you become.

In order to earn people's trust, you have to know them. More important, they have to really feel that you know them and genuinely care about them. In fact, trust is the most important characteristic of an influential and intimate relationship. In the context of a business relationship, trust comes from a sincere conviction in the hearts and minds of your colleagues that you are working in their best interest and that you really know what their best interest is. Once you gain an understanding of what really matters to the business, it's time to come up with strategic responses to their issues.[2]

I recently met with Michael Del Priore, the vice president and global CIO of Church & Dwight Company, the leading U.S. producer of baking soda. Founded in 1846, the company is best known for its Arm & Hammer brand, one of the nation's most trusted trademarks. It also makes a variety of other consumer and specialty products and operates internationally. Michael joined the company in the summer of 2009 and determined that the organization required a strategic-planning process, a governance model, and an organizational structure to partner with the business.

In response, Michael spearheaded an initiative to build a strategic plan for IT. He began by interviewing top executives and other business stakeholders across the company. "The interviews helped me introduce the 'voice of the customer' into the planning process with my team," he says. Michael then spent a few months with his team to document a three-year plan and validate it with senior business leaders. Afterward, he conducted a town hall meeting with his full staff to announce the details. "A main theme of our plan was to transition from having country-specific IT to having a global IT organization, including platforms, processes, tools, and a new organizational structure," he explains.

As a transformational CIO, Michael appreciates the importance of creating a governance framework and integrating IT into the decision-making process:

> *We didn't want to be in a situation where the business makes a request and we just react to it. We wanted our account managers to be integrated into the process and help develop the concepts and ideas. Having a documented strategic plan helps establish the context for making decisions on specific projects.*

Setting Priorities

After becoming a trusted partner with the business, you can raise the ante and seek to become part of the priority-setting process at the operational level—the second stage of building partnership. The key here is to get your lieutenants to have a voice in the priority-setting operational committees. This stage helps you progress from order taking to priority setting.

A best practice is to create committees for each of your major business processes, such as sales, customer service, and accounting. These teams should consist of individuals from all across the company rather than being monopolized by corporate stakeholders. Assign an IT relationship manager to each of these committees to partake in discussions to help set priorities related to business processes. The IT relationship managers should have a full vote on proposals presented to the committees—accept nothing less. IT is in an excellent position to judge proposals, given its breadth of exposure to all major business processes and priorities.

Ken Harris is the CIO of Shaklee, the top natural nutrition company in the United States and the leading provider of premium-quality natural nutrition products, personal-care products, and environmentally friendly home-care products. With more than 1.2 million members and distributors around the globe, Shaklee currently operates in the United States, Mexico, Canada, Japan, Malaysia, Taiwan, and China.

Ken is a celebrated CIO with more than 25 years of success leading IT at high-profile companies such as Gap, Nike, and Pepsi-Cola. I recently caught up with Ken to ask about his view on setting priorities with the business. Here is what he told me:

> *It is imperative to have a prioritization process so that your department is working off the same sheet of music with the rest of the business. At*

Shaklee, we have two distinct but interrelated processes for setting priority and aligning with the business. The first is an IT strategic-planning process involving the executive management team. We meet on a monthly basis to review progress on existing initiatives, prioritize new opportunities, and calibrate the budget. The second process involves weekly meetings with the people at the next level down in the organization where we discuss progress and issues at a more tactical level. The process of communicating both at the executive and operational level on a frequent basis creates a level of intimacy necessary for developing a strong business partnership.

Maintaining a productive relationship with your business partners through frequent contact points appears to be an effective method to align on priorities for technology-enabled business initiatives. I met with other CIOs who share this philosophy.

Greg Fell is the CIO at Terex Corporation, a diversified global manufacturer in five business segments: aerial work platforms, construction, cranes, material handling and port solutions, and materials processing. Terex manufactures a broad range of equipment for use in various industries. Terex also offers financial products and services to assist in the acquisition of Terex equipment through Terex Financial Services. I recently got together with Greg and asked him to describe the IT governance practices at the company. Here is what he said:

An ERP system is less about technology transformation and more about business-process transformation. So when we began our ERP initiative here at Terex, we created a governance process that involved meeting with the business executives every other week for two hours to review progress and priorities. The frequency and amount of time we spend together has helped create awareness of the opportunities and challenges that we need to collaborate on. Now when projects cost a bit more or take longer than initially expected, the leadership team has a better understanding and appreciation of the issues. The meetings also help drive the ownership of the issues. And in many cases, issue resolution is owned by individuals outside IT.

It is important to ensure that every project in your portfolio has a measurable business case and is aligned with company goals. The committees can also be effective bodies for developing long-term strategic plans that represent the key objectives for each process area. Another important factor is that the committees should all be managed by a singular governance framework. The framework should be thoroughly documented and describe the purpose and process of setting priorities and objectives in support of company strategies and goals. See Chapter 3 for more detail on developing a governance framework.

Creating Business Strategy

The final and most coveted stage in the IT—business partnership is for IT to be viewed as a venerable part of the business. At this stage, IT and the business converge and are indistinguishable. To achieve this step, the IT leader in your company needs to sit on the steering committee responsible for creating the vision, goals, and strategies for the business. This committee provides the guidance and parameters for the priority-setting committees discussed earlier, since all priorities should be aligned with the company's overarching vision, goals, and strategies.

Getting a seat on the steering committee is not always easy, since IT still has an image problem in many organizations. IT has to get out from underneath the oppressive rock of being viewed as simply a service provider and transform into a true business partner. This is accomplished by demonstrating success with partnering and consistently delivering on the objectives defined by you and your peers. Remember, trust is *earned*—it's an achieved privilege, not an entitlement. Once your CEO sees that you can be counted on to deliver value consistent with the company's core vision, you will begin to earn your rightful seat at the table.

Rich Brennen is a partner at Spencer Stuart, one of the world's leading executive-search consulting firms. Rich built Spencer Stuart's global information officer practice and served as its global leader for over a decade. He has recruited more than 250 CIOs, including the top IT executives for the Walt Disney Company, the Allstate Corporation, Barclays, CIGNA, the Clorox Company, Juniper Networks, State Street, Kimberly-Clark, Walgreen's, and the Kroger Company.

I asked Rich to describe the qualities of a transformational CIO. Here is what he said:

> *Trying to describe a transformational CIO is like trying to describe a cloud. It's amorphous and depends on the view of the person describing it. For instance, one client may describe a transformational CIO as someone who*

can move their back-office IT to be more front and center in the business. Another client may describe it as someone who can help reduce IT costs or fix a failed outsourcing arrangement.

There is no rigorous definition of a transformational CIO, although there are certain themes that we keep hearing today from companies seeking new CIOs. The first is the CIO must be laser focused on the business. The new CIO role is as much of a business executive as the head of manufacturing, sales, supply chain, or any other function. Another theme is that clients are requesting a CIO who has run a business unit in the past or at a minimum has had some non-IT experience.

The best CIOs are indistinguishable from the other business executives in the room. If you were a fly on the wall listening to a discussion between the CIO and other CXOs for thirty minutes, you would not be able to identify the CIO as he or she is speaking about business outcomes and achieving business strategies. It's the CIO's job to leverage technology to enable the business, and the best CIOs discuss opportunities and challenges in business terms, not technical terms.

I met with Susan Miller, the CIO of a major sports franchise. Susan shares an interesting perspective on earning a seat at the table with the company's other executives. Here is what she told me:

When I joined the company several years ago, I had two major initiatives that I needed to address right from the start. The first was to transition from a decentralized IT organization to a shared service organization, including a new infrastructure platform. The second was to move headquarters into a new office building in Chicago that we had to design from top to bottom. The shared service initiative was an internal IT restructuring effort coupled with a technical architecture upgrade, requiring little involvement from the business. The new office building project involved having us work very closely with the business to design the layout of the new space and even the selection of the furniture—all of which required heavy interaction with the rest of the leadership team.

CIOs need to be comfortable with both ends of the spectrum. In one moment they may be working on a disaster recovery project with their team, and in the next moment they could be sitting next to the CEO working on the business plan. What people don't often realize is that success with the low-profile projects, such as higher network bandwidth, actually helps you earn the trust and credibility needed to gain a seat at the table with the rest of the business executives.

| Trust is *earned*—it's an achieved privilege, not an entitlement.

I sat down with David Kaufman, the CIO of Aramark Corporation, a leader in professional services providing award-winning food services, facilities management, and uniform and career apparel to health-care institutions, universities and school districts, stadiums and arenas, and businesses around the world. In *Fortune* magazine's 2011 list of the World's Most Admired Companies, Aramark was ranked number one in its industry. Since 1998 it has consistently ranked as one of the top three most admired companies in its industry, as evaluated by peers and analysts.

David views strategic planning as a bottom up–top down process involving the development of an annualized portfolio of initiatives. He meets with the strategic committee, composed of people who directly report to the CEO, on a quarterly basis to review progress toward goals and set priorities and sequencing for each new initiative. As David describes it, "The quarterly presentations typically include a review of whether the initiative is on time, on budget, and producing the desired business outcomes. We also discuss the risks and mitigation plans for each of the initiatives."

The key is illustrating how IT fits into the company's core vision. There are many ways of illustrating IT's alignment with the company's vision, but perhaps the best approach lies with developing a balanced scorecard and strategy map. In *Strategy Maps*, business strategy consultants Robert S. Kaplan and David P. Norton explained that strategy maps are a way to provide a uniform and consistent way to describe strategy, so that objectives and measures can be established and managed. A strategy map describes the logic of the strategy, showing clearly the objectives for the internal processes that create value and the intangible assets required to support them. The balanced scorecard translates the strategy-map objectives into measures and targets. But objectives and targets will not be achieved simply because they have been identified; the organization must launch a set of actionable programs that will enable the targets for all of the measures to be achieved.[3]

Establishing a governance framework helps IT to identify and prioritize projects across the major business initiatives and processes.

Due to the very nature of their jobs, CIOs inherit many projects as a result of partnering with their business peers. Documenting the objectives in the form of a strategic plan will help you describe how IT contributes to company strategy.

Develop an IT Strategic Plan

The planning process helps you to create and communicate your vision and allow people to understand their purpose in the organization. I recently attended the World Business Forum in New York City, where Gary Burnison, the CEO of Korn/Ferry International, a global leader in executive recruitment, gave a talk on talent management. Gary says that the number one reason people leave companies is that they don't understand how they matter. No one has told them how they fit in. He adds, "In this era, when self-interest trumps mutual interest, leadership defines how people fit into the journey."

In *Motivate Like a CEO*, Suzanne Bates wrote, "As a leader, you have to learn how to communicate mission and purpose so that it makes sense to every single person in the organization. This can be challenging. You really have to get to know the individual and the group so you understand how to make the purpose relevant, exciting, and motivating for them. People need to see how they fit into the larger mission of the organization."[4]

I spoke with John Hinkle, the CIO of Take-Two Interactive Software Inc., a leading developer, marketer, and publisher of interactive entertainment for consumers around the globe. The company develops and publishes products through its two wholly-owned labels, Rockstar Games and 2K; 2K publishes its titles under the 2K Games, 2K Sports, and 2K Play brands. The company publishes such popular game franchises as Grand Theft Auto, Midnight Club, Red Dead Redemption, Max Payne, Bully, and Manhunt.

John believes it is important to connect the *why* with the *what* for his staff:

> *If one of my project managers is giving an update on a global network upgrade, you can always count on me to chime in and explain how the project is adding value to the business. I might say something like "The*

upgrade will mean that we can reduce the time it takes to transfer the latest game build to the QA Lab by 70 percent and save thousands of dollars in lost QA productivity.'' When people have an understanding of why they are doing something, they tend to become more motivated to achieve the goal. I want people who work for me to understand why they are working on something and, more important, love what they are doing. If you just want to punch a clock, then I don't have a role for you here.

People need to see how they fit into the larger mission of the organization.

I recently caught up with Jim Gerry, the vice president of North America IT at Hyatt Hotels Corporation, a leading global hospitality company with a proud heritage of making guests feel more than welcome. The company's subsidiaries manage, franchise, own, and develop hotels and resorts under the Hyatt, Park Hyatt, Andaz, Grand Hyatt, Hyatt Regency, Hyatt Place, and Hyatt Summerfield Suites brand names and have locations on six continents.

Jim works with his team and business leadership to develop a five-year strategic plan. He feels strongly about vetting the plan with the executives and functional constituents at Hyatt so that everyone has a voice in influencing the IT strategies and objectives:

We have quarterly business reviews with the CEO and his direct reports to review progress toward current-year plans and how initiatives align with the five-year strategic plan. On a semiannual basis, we conduct an IT steering committee meeting with functional heads across the company to review current programs, projects, and priorities. This process helps to ensure that everyone understands the big initiatives and has a chance to weigh in.

The participants in these sessions have the opportunity to share what they think is working well, not working well, or what we should be working on. I have learned throughout my career that even the most well-thought-out strategic plans will need to change on a periodic basis to address changes in the business climate. What's important is you have multiple channels to listen to your team and your business stakeholders and adapt your plan accordingly.

How to Get Started

The purpose of an IT strategic plan is to define, in cooperation with the relevant stakeholders, how IT will contribute to the company's goals and the related costs and risks over time—usually three to five years. It includes how IT will help the business meet its goals and objectives by translating business requirements into technology products and service offerings while being transparent about benefits, costs, and risks.

An IT strategic plan typically includes:

- A strategic-planning process
- IT's vision, mission, and goals
- The company's vision, goals, and values
- Mapping business initiatives to business goals
- Mapping IT strategies to business initiatives
- Mapping IT objectives to IT strategies
- Categorizing IT objectives by domain (business and technical)
- IT benchmarking study results
- IT trends
- Measuring progress toward IT goals
- IT spending

The Sections of an IT Strategic Plan

Let's examine each of these sections to further describe the content to help you get started on your own IT strategic plan.

The Strategic-Planning Process. Strategy is not a stand-alone process; it is one step in a logical continuum that moves an organization from a high-level mission statement to the work performed by frontline and back-office employees.[5] The development of an IT strategic plan should be managed as a project by the IT leadership team and include input from key stakeholders, staff members, and opinion leaders in the company.

A plan can be developed using six activities:

1. Defining the purpose of the plan
2. Capturing and evaluating business needs
3. Assessing the ability to support the needs
4. Developing the plan and the key performance indicators
5. Validating the plan
6. Communicating the plan

The project is followed by the ongoing activities of monitoring, governing, and managing to achieve the anticipated results.

IT's Vision, Mission, and Goals. Just as a company has a vision, a mission, and a set of goals, individual departments should create their own maxims to articulate how they fit into the overall picture. See Chapter 2 for more information on how to brand your department and set a vision, a mission, and a set of goals.

The Company's Vision, Goals, and Values. It's always helpful for the readers of your plan to be able to easily reference the company's vision, goals, and values. This way, it's clear to them that IT is aligned with the rest of the organization and not marching down a different path.

Mapping Business Initiatives to Business Goals. The next step is to have a clear understanding of how the business initiatives (e.g., a new marketing campaign) link to a business goal. This is where the planning process gets interesting. Unfortunately, many organizations do not take the time to document business goals, let alone business initiatives. Even some Fortune 500 companies haven't inked more than a vision and mission statement. Of course, this makes it difficult for individual departments to align their initiatives to the business.

If you find yourself in this situation, approach it as an excellent opportunity to exhibit your business chops and partnering abilities. Recruit the assistance of your direct reporters and process committees to document business goals and initiatives from their perspective. I have been able to use this grassroots strategy to influence corporate leadership teams to develop strategic plans, or at least convince other department heads to document their individual plans. You may ruffle a few feathers along the way, but people will eventually realize you have the best interests of the company at heart—and they will also become convinced that you're not just a technologist. Once you have the goals and initiatives documented, you can move on to the next step: to link IT strategies to the business initiatives.

Mapping IT Strategies to Business Initiatives. In this step, your objective is to define one or more IT strategies that can support each business initiative. For instance, if a business initiative is to launch a new consumer product, then you can describe IT strategies in support of that business initiative. The strategy is at a high level and does not describe the details to fulfill the requirements of the initiative—that is in the next step. To use the example of the launch of a consumer product we will call XYZ, an IT strategy might go something like this: Partner with the operational functions to provide the technology products and services in support of XYZ product launch.

Mapping IT Objectives to IT Strategies. Once you have all of your IT strategies documented, you can have your direct reports work with their teams to define the specific objectives for the next three to five years that will be used to address the strategies, further describing the IT partnership with the business. The objectives describe realistic targets for the strategy and should be developed using the SMART method. SMART is an acronym for *specific, measurable, achievable, relevant,* and *time framed,* the five leading measures of a strong objective—a realistic target for the strategy. The first-known use of the term was by George T. Doran in the November 1981 issue of *Management Review.*

As discussed earlier, it is important to help employees understand how they fit into the big picture. This task is accomplished by setting SMART objectives and assigning the objectives to individuals who will be responsible for executing them. In this way, the IT strategic plan and the individual performance plans are confluent. It's also a good practice to meet with your business partners and direct reporters on a periodic basis to recalibrate the strategies and objectives.

Setting SMART objectives aligns individual development plans with the strategic plan.

Categorizing IT Objectives by Domain (Business and Technical). It is helpful to classify IT objectives into specific business-application or technical domains so you can analyze your portfolio according to the domains. The strategic plan doesn't just focus on business applications; it also includes the supporting infrastructure objectives. By classifying objectives into domains, you can see how the objectives from various functional areas can form a collection of actions that address a strategic outcome for the company.

For instance, an IT department may have one function to support sales objectives and another function to support customer service, even though the objectives are part of customer relationship management. Customer relationship management entails all aspects of interaction that a company has with its customers, whether they are sales or service related. By grouping specific objectives in the sales and service functions as part of that domain, you can analyze how you are addressing the needs of the customer.

Here is a list of examples of domains to consider for your strategic plan:

Business Application Domains
- Enterprise resource planning (ERP)
- Customer relationship management (CRM)
- Supply chain management (SCM)
- Human capital management (HCM)
- Business intelligence (BI)

Technical Domains
- Software architecture
- Database
- Server
- Storage
- Desktop

- Messaging
- Networking and telecommunications

IT Benchmarking Study Results. A popular way for IT departments to identify opportunity for improvement and competitive advantage is to compare its performance with other companies through benchmarking. It's helpful to include a summary of the benchmarking study results in your strategic plan to give readers an understanding of your strategies in relation to competitors or other companies of similar size. See Chapter 2 for a description of how to conduct a benchmarking study.

IT Trends. The purpose of the next step in the strategic plan is to describe the trends in the IT industry: the critical issues, opportunities, and challenges that all organizations face. The trends help IT departments make informed strategic and tactical decisions to better serve the needs of the business.

As part of the strategic-planning process, CIOs should have their function heads research the key trends for their area (i.e., the business application domains listed earlier). The following is a list of technology categories that serve as suggested areas of study for trends that are likely to have an impact on IT products and services:

- Application development and integration
- Business-process management
- Cloud computing
- Consumer technologies
- Data management and data integration
- IT asset management
- IT management, operations, and services
- Mobile and wireless devices
- Networking and communications equipment and services
- PCs, laptops, and handheld devices
- Regulatory compliance

- Security and privacy
- Servers and storage
- Social networking

Use this section of your strategic plan to document several trends for each of these categories and include a summary statement for each category. Encourage your IT function heads to identify the trends by leveraging a multitude of sources, including white papers from IT research and advisory companies, technology journals, publications, websites, conferences, and seminars.

Measuring Progress toward IT Goals. As part of the planning process, it's important to define ways to measure progress toward business and IT goals. Key performance indicators (KPIs) are quantifiable measurements that reflect the critical success factors of a company or individual department.

Whether you decide on the traditional written form or a graphical representation of your plan, what is important is that it is easily understood and embraced by your business partners and staff. It should also be documented in a way that can be easily updated, since things change quite frequently in the IT industry. A sample template for a strategic plan is available on the companion website.

Key Performance Indicators for IT Goals. Here is an example of KPIs that can be considered for an IT department:

- **Delivery.** The product or service is implemented on time and within budget and meets business requirements. This is typically measured by comparing the final delivery date with the delivery date that was agreed on with the user.
- **User satisfaction.** Users of the product or service are satisfied. This is typically measured by user satisfaction surveys.
- **Number and severity of defects.** To ensure that IT delivers quality products and services, evaluate the number and severity of defects (issues) with the product or service delivered.
- **Number of controls passed.** IT is required to adhere to specific controls to ensure that its computer systems generate accurate

financial reports; for publicly traded companies, Sarbanes-Oxley controls are specified by auditors. This KPI measures the numbers of controls passed as part of implementing a product.

- **Savings.** This KPI measures the monetary savings obtained by implementing a product or service. A benefit analysis will be defined up front and measured as part of the delivery of the product or service.
- **Revenues.** This KPI measures the revenue earned by implementing a product or service. A benefit analysis will also be defined up front and measured as part of the delivery of the product or service.
- **Efficiencies.** An important measurement is the improvement with operational efficiencies. A productivity analysis will be defined up front and measured as part of the delivery of the product and or service.
- **Competitive advantage.** A difficult but important indicator to measure is the level of competitive advantage gained by a product or service. A practical method of examining the level of success with this indicator is through benchmarking.
- **Business alignment.** In order for IT to maximize and sustain its value to the business, it must ensure that it is aligned with organizational goals and objectives. This indicator is measured through the IT governance framework (e.g., voting or surveys).
- **Transparency.** This indicator measures how IT communicates the scope, progress, risks, milestones, and achievements that are related to an objective. Typically, instruments such as project status reports, scorecards, and annual reports are used for this purpose.
- **Availability.** This indicator focuses on the operational health and stability without which IT will be unable to establish credibility with its users. From a user's perspective, a primary concern relates to application and service availability. This indicator is measured by the performance against the IT service level agreement.
- **Security incidents.** Security incidents are becoming significant for IT organizations. Whether they are viruses, spam, denial of service attacks, or hacker penetrations or come in some other form, security breaches have an impact on business. This indicator is measured by

the number and severity of incidents—particularly any incident that leads to adverse monetary costs in lost revenues, recovery costs, and even fines.

- **Employee turnover.** This is the ratio of the number of IT workers who had to be replaced in a given period to the average number of workers in the same period.

Key Performance Indicators for Business Goals. Delivering IT products and services on time and within budget will definitely earn you credibility, but how do you transform your role so you're more than a technologist? In this section, you will learn how to capitalize on the information stored in the systems to measure performance and influence business outcomes. There is no other role or department in a company with such an inimitable ability to harvest data across multiple business domains to demonstrate results with cross-functional initiatives. So leverage your technical strengths to convey your business leadership abilities.

CIOs can stand out and create real value by helping their business partners identify and measure KPIs for each of the business goals. Business leaders typically focus most, if not all, of their attention on business results, including revenue, profit, and customer satisfaction. These results are vital to every company, regardless of industry, geography, and size. Business results are linked to the performance of employees, products, services, and market conditions. However, surprisingly, there is typically less focus on the KPIs that drive these business results. For instance, the amount of time that sales representatives spend following up with their leads can be a KPI.

CIOs can stand out and create real value by helping their business partners identify and measure KPIs.

KPIs are measurements of performance and are used to periodically assess the performance of divisions, departments, and employees. They are specific, measurable, controllable, and meaningful. KPIs are linked to targeted values, so measurements can be taken several times and assessed as meeting expectations or not.

When companies develop and measure KPIs, they typically confine them to individual business processes (e.g., sales, marketing, or purchasing), instead of combining the KPIs into one cohesive and holistic scorecard. Having one scorecard for all of the KPIs allows business leaders to examine the correlation between the measurements and get more of a holistic view of the operations. This approach creates an immense transparency of the company's performance. It's also a great way to exhibit your interest and abilities in gathering and reporting on business measurements.

As a CIO, you are in a unique position to identify, analyze, and report on KPIs across the business. You probably already have a data warehouse that collects most of the data needed for this purpose. It's now a matter of partnering with your business peers to establish the appropriate KPIs for each function and the expected performance threshold for each indicator. Be sure to leverage the governance committees for this activity. Also, tap into the BI experience of your staff members to help you design reports and scorecards to communicate the results. Helping your company move the ball with operational KPIs will showcase your business acumen and your interest in improving business results.

Conclusion. When you achieve the three stages of building a business partnership described in this chapter—earning trust, setting priorities, and creating business strategy—you will have reached an inflection point in your career. You will become a trusted business leader capable of discussing business issues, defining company strategies, and delivering business outcomes along with your peers in other departments.

IT Spending. No IT strategic plan is complete without a forecast of expense and capital spending for each IT group (e.g., infrastructure or development). The forecast also includes head-count projections.

I realize that I have repeatedly mentioned the time frame for a strategic plan to be three to five years and the challenge that poses for an IT organization, given the pace of change in technology. Some would argue that two years is a more practical time frame for an IT plan. It really depends on the expectations of the leadership team. If every other department is being asked to project for five years, however, it is difficult to argue in favor of a shorter time frame for IT merely because of the volatility in technology. My point is that if the other departments are asked to forecast for five years, there is no sense in arguing it—it may even help stretch your thinking in terms of trends.

Different Approaches to Strategic Planning

There really isn't one way of developing a strategic plan. Gary Boyd is the CIO of Windsor Health Group, a managed health-care company operating government-sponsored health plans and providing specialty managed-care services to both the insurance and health-care provider communities. Gary has a very unique approach to strategic planning that is worth describing.

Every year, the three divisions at Windsor update their business plans based on the strategic goals of the company. Gary and his team are involved in helping to influence the business plans. Once the business plans are updated, IT then produces its own strategic plan that is aligned with the divisions. However, that is when things get interesting. You see, Gary doesn't write a strategic plan, he *draws* it. Instead of a creating a written narrative describing the IT initiatives that support the business plan, Gary develops a blueprint, a visual representation of his plan, the target landscape, and how it ties directly to supporting the strategic goals:

> *The blueprint has four layers for each plan year, including applications, integration points, data repositories, and information exploitation. It has been an invaluable tool in helping me communicate how IT is enabling the business plan. Our goal is to ensure that everyone in the organization has a clear view of the IT priorities and their tie-in with the business growth enablers. The blueprints depict a clear migration path that describes what capabilities need to be introduced, and how. Of course change is possible—and managing change in any environment has its challenges; this is why we have a clear change management process in place that allows us to fine-tune our direction during the course of the year.*

Differentiate Customers and Partners

Before I end this chapter, it's important that I address an age-old issue. Time after time, I hear IT executives and their staff members refer to employees in their companies as their *customers*. This is a monumental mistake, and it should be averted at all costs. I know the term may be viewed as mere lexicon, but it is one of the reasons so many IT departments are still looked down on as "service providers" instead of treated as equal business partners.

Your Real Customer. Let's be clear: Your customers are the institutions or individuals purchasing your company's products and services; company employees are *not* your customers. If you refer to the employees in your company as your customers, you will never achieve a real partnership with them, and you will remain an order taker—subservient to other departmental employees. Also, don't attempt to soften the term by using *internal customer*. It does nothing to help you gain parity with your business peers.

Think about it this way: When was the last time your company's chief financial officer (CFO) referred to employees in other departments as his or her customers? In my 26-year career, I have yet to hear a CFO, a chief marketing officer (CMO), a chief operating officer (COO), or any other department head refer to employees as customers. I have also never heard any of them yearning to "align with the business," for that matter. Yet these other departments provide services to the organization. Let's face it, every department provides services to the organization. We are all in it together, so don't denigrate and segregate your IT staff from the rest of the business—unless you want to be viewed as a vendor.

> Your customers are the institutions or individuals purchasing your company's products and services; company employees are *not* your customers.

When I worked for Pepsi-Cola in the late 1990s, the CIO at the time lived by the ideology that employees should never be considered customers. At the time, I thought it was a bit eccentric, and I honestly didn't pay much heed to it. Over time, though, I began to realize the significance of what he meant—usually when I came across a business peer who arrogantly believed that he or she was my superior and I was there to *serve* him or her. I recall reflecting on the value that my team and I were providing to the organization and to our *real* customers, and I realized the employees were my business partners, not my customers. I just had to educate my business peer on the terms of our relationship.

Ten years later I attended a *CIO* magazine conference where the then-retired CIO of Pepsi-Cola (who went on to run IT at Dell) happened to be giving a talk. During his presentation, he unremittingly hit on the same points about the importance of treating business colleagues as your partners, not as your customers. I was fascinated by the fact that he held on to his ideology for all those years. At that point, I was convinced, through his unwavering belief and from my own experiences, that he was absolutely right. From that moment on, I became resolute that the only customers IT professionals should recognize are the ones buying their company's products and services.

Earn Your Right to Be a Partner. I met with Jon Harding, the CIO of Conair Corporation, a developer, manufacturer, and marketer of health and beauty products and kitchen and electronic appliances. Jon believes that a CIO has to earn the right to be a business partner by executing on the fundamentals:

> *In general, I do see employees in other departments as partners in the sense that we consult with them on how to capitalize on technology to drive operational efficiencies and revenue opportunities. As an example, we are currently migrating back-office processes from South America to the United States. While the technology change involved in the effort is relatively low, there is significant change with respect to business processes and people, which we have been able to consult on. When change is met with resistance, however, IT's ability to influence business stakeholders rests on how well it executes on fundamentals, such as system uptime. If you are trying to drive change in the business, but you haven't provided good technology services, you will not earn the right to be a partner.*

Take on Responsibilities Outside of IT

Consider broadening your value to the business by applying your leadership skills and business knowledge to other areas. According to *CIO* magazine's "2012 State of the CIO Survey," 57 percent of the CIOs surveyed are responsible for one or more non-IT areas of the business.

The most commonly added functions include security, strategy, risk management, administration or operations, and customer service.

Opportunities Await You. Don't wait for your boss to come knocking on your office door to offer you responsibilities outside of IT. If you're interested in gaining more business experience, then go ask for more responsibilities. Look for opportunities where your skills and experiences complement the duties that you are interested in obtaining.

If you have never held a position outside of IT before, then I suggest you start with something that has close ties with your experience. For instance, customer service is a great place to start, because you inevitably have a background in managing IT as a shared service organization for your company. Your familiarity with service technologies and processes will give you a leg up with taking on responsibility in this area. It will also help you become more familiar with your company's products, which can open up even more doors later.

Don't Be Afraid to Create Opportunities. In some cases, you can even *create* opportunities for non–IT responsibilities. A good example is when IT is involved in business-process reengineering efforts. In most of these cases, IT becomes intimately involved in identifying, defining, documenting, and training in the standardized processes. Once the standardized processes are in place, business-process owners typically go back to their day jobs, leaving IT to support the processes and the systems.

Even if business functional heads are officially assigned the responsibility of being process owners, they typically fall out of touch with the details of the processes because they usually are not involved in providing day-to-day support. As time goes on and the process owners become more and more engrossed in their day jobs, the need for a dedicated process owner emerges—especially if the company is interested in continuously improving processes and systems. In these instances, CIOs are in a perfect position to step up and volunteer to take on process leadership for the organization.

Don't be surprised if you are met with some resistance—your business partners may not want to give up the title, even though they may not have the time to perform the duties. Also, there is still a stigma in many companies that IT is all about the "techy stuff" and is not familiar enough with the business practices—even though IT is responsible for supporting and training employees in the intricate details of the operational processes. It may take some influencing on your part, but if you want to be seen as a business leader, consider taking on more than just technical responsibilities. The opportunities exist (or can be created), but you need to be the one knocking on doors.

Brian R. Lurie is the senior vice president and CIO of Teleflex, a global provider of medical devices used in critical care and surgery. Teleflex serves health-care providers in more than 130 countries with specialty devices for vascular access, general and regional anesthesia, urology, respiratory care, cardiac care, and surgery. Teleflex also provides products and services for device manufacturers.

I met with Brian to get his view on CIOs taking on responsibilities outside of IT. Brian believes that while CIOs are in a great position to take on broader business responsibilities, they shouldn't get caught up with needing to *own* other functions. He believes that CIOs can create additional value for the business by simply identifying and promoting opportunities for improvement in other functions:

> *Since IT touches most of the business functions in an organization, it's in a unique position to connect the dots and identify opportunities. While I don't presently have responsibilities outside of IT, I have gotten involved in developing programs that are well beyond IT. For instance, I created a reward and recognition program and a talent management program that are now used across the global company. In both of these cases, human resources ended up owning the programs, but IT was a catalyst in initiating them.*

Cloud Computing Is Changing the Role of IT

I have been careful to write a book that will stand the test of time by not being trendy. With this in mind, I don't think that cloud computing is merely a fad that will last a few years and be replaced with a new paradigm. Cloud computing will be at the forefront of computing for many years to come and will change the role of IT for the better. For this reason, I am including a section dedicated to this topic to help IT professionals better prepare for this evolving shift in how technology products and services are delivered.

The growing popularity of cloud computing raises a fundamental issue for IT leaders: How do we stay relevant? As the IT organization transitions from being the owner and operator of internal infrastructure and business applications to a role that involves managing a more complex multiplatform mix of internal and external services, CIOs are tasked with redefining IT's value to the business. The shift is well underway. In a recent global market pulse survey of IT managers in the United States and Europe, 96 percent of the respondents acknowledged that IT's primary role has changed over the past five years, and 40 percent of those believed it has changed to a great extent.[6]

What's driving the change? The survey found that process standardization, increased automation, and a rise in outsourcing engagements—including moving more services to the cloud—have all contributed to the transition. In the market pulse survey, sponsored by CA Technologies and conducted by IDG Research Services, more than two-thirds (71 percent) of IT managers believed that cloud computing will continue to change the role of IT.[7]

So how do you not only survive the cloud but thrive along with it? Let's take a look at some of the jobs that will disappear, so we can help our staff members better prepare for the eventual transition. The jobs that will go away in the not-too-distant future include help desk technicians, as desktops become very thin appliances, and network administrators, since many of their day-to-day responsibilities will no longer be required as companies outsource their server applications. The hosting provider will take care of all of the server backups and maintenance, so you won't need to have that staff on hand.

In contrast, the jobs that will become more important include network engineering, security, relationship management, contract law and negotiation, and process management. These are discussed in the following sections.

Network Engineering

The very nature of cloud computing means that organizations will be absolutely dependent on Internet connectivity. If connectivity to the outside world fails, the entire cloud computing model breaks. I expect organizations to hire network engineers whose job it will be to ensure optimal connectivity. Network engineers will have to focus on ensuring network reliability as their top priority. I also expect traffic shaping to become a hot skill for engineers. Traffic shaping, if you aren't familiar with it, is a science that deals with prioritizing network bandwidth.[8]

Security

Another major growth area will be security, and most organizations' security needs are likely to change. After all, server-level security becomes a nonissue if you don't have any servers. Likewise, desktop security—at least by its current definition—will go away as bloated desktop operating systems give way to bootable thin-client components. Network security will become vitally important, even more so than it is now. Not only will organizations have to prevent packet sniffing on the network, they will also have to take measures to prevent denial-of-service (DoS) attacks. Bandwidth saturation has the potential to be the Achilles's heel of cloud computing, so a DoS attack could prove to be crippling.[9]

Relationship Management

While we may see more users forming direct relationships with cloud vendors for specialty applications that are not at the company's core business, organizations will continue to rely on IT relationship managers for the strategic applications and services. With that in mind, interpersonal skills are critical for success. Candidates for relationship manager roles must be excellent analytical thinkers and problem solvers as well as effective communicators.

Contract Law and Negotiation

Since the very nature of cloud computing means that a company will rely more heavily on outsourcing operations to a third-party supplier, companies will need people who are experienced on how to create and maintain contracts. Of course, if a company chooses a private cloud computing deployment model, then that becomes less of an issue. However, most companies have some level of a hybrid deployment model in place, which involves private and public cloud computing. If you and your direct reports don't have much experience with outsourcing, take time to study the topic, since it will become a larger slice of the IT portfolio.

Process Management

In order to succeed with a cloud project, service level management, configuration management, and change management will require much of your attention. If your IT team already follows a proven methodology like Microsoft Operations Framework or the IT infrastructure library, it will give you a leg up with implementing a cloud project.

In addition, IT managers must understand the integration between cloud architecture and existing processes. When a cloud service has been integrated into business processes, it gets to be a part of the business instead of a solitary silo. This does not mean that cloud projects will not deliver change to these processes. Shifting services, infrastructure, or applications to the cloud implies changing how those processes work.[10]

> CIOs will be measured on how well they transition from being the owners and operators of internal technologies to managing a multitude of vendors who are integrated into IT's value chain.

To successfully manage a rollout of cloud-based applications, infrastructure, and services, organizations need to carefully identify and plan for a new set of skills. Some of these skills can be provisioned by simply retooling existing employees through training. In other cases, companies will need to recruit employees who already have the skills in place. This will depend on the timing of new cloud initiatives.

What's clear is that CIOs will be measured on how well they transition from being the owners and operators of internal technologies to managing a multitude of vendors who are integrated into IT's value chain. If this transition is executed well, users will not be able to tell the difference between products and services that are provided internally versus externally.

Top Plays

- Once you have demonstrated that you can be relied on to deliver value to the company, you become a trusted partner.
- Enlist your lieutenants to be on priority-setting committees with their business peers.
- Communicate often with your business partners to create professional intimacy.
- Make sure your project portfolio is aligned with company goals.
- Illustrate IT's alignment with the company's vision using a strategy map.
- Use the six activities described in this chapter to build an IT strategic plan:
  1. Defining the purpose of the plan
  2. Capturing and evaluating business needs
  3. Assessing the ability to support the needs
  4. Developing the plan and the KPIs
  5. Validating the plan
  6. Communicating the plan
- Develop and measure the KPIs that drive business results.
- Employees in other departments are your business partners, not your customers.
- Expand your role by taking on responsibilities outside of IT.
- Prepare your staff for the transition to cloud computing.

Notes

1. Neil Rackham, Lawrence Friedman, and Richard Ruff, *Getting Partnering Right: How Market Leaders Are Creating Long-Term Competitive Advantage* (New York: McGraw-Hill, 1996), 12–13.

2. Marc J. Schiller, *The 11 Secrets of Highly Influential IT Leaders* (Mamaroneck, NY: privately printed, 2011), 47.

3. Robert S. Kaplan and David P. Norton, *Strategy Maps: Converting Intangible Assets into Tangible Outcomes* (Boston: Harvard Business School Publishing, 2004), 29–55.

4. Suzanne Bates, *Motivate Like a CEO: Communicate Your Strategic Vision and Inspire People to Act!* (New York: McGraw-Hill, 2009), 13.

5. Kaplan and Norton, *Strategy Maps.*

6. "With a Push from Cloud Computing IT Shifts toward Supply Chain," Computer Associates, *Market Pulse*, white paper, p. 1, www.ca.com/~/media/Files/whitepapers/final_paper_idg_role_of_it.pdf.

7. *Ibid.*

8. Brien Posey, "IT Cloud Survival Skills." *Redmond*, May 1, 2010.

9. *Ibid.*

10. Jrliem, "New Skills Required for Cloud Computing Success," *Cloud Computing*, September 16, 2011, http://cloudcomputingx.org/new-skills-for-cloud-computing-success.html.

Chapter 2

Step 2: Organize

By failing to prepare, you are preparing to fail.

—*Benjamin Franklin*

Organize: Define the organizational structure and processes needed to run IT effectively and efficiently so that it delivers value-added products and services, seeks continuous improvement, and is prepared to adapt to business change.

Once you have developed a partnership with your business colleagues, it's time to organize your department so you can deliver the anticipated results. I avoid using the phrase "run IT like a business" because it implies that the people inside your company are your customers. Instead, IT professionals should aspire to be more businesslike in their planning, processes, investment analysis, project management, measurement, and behavior. This chapter focuses on the practices of defining the IT mission, vision, goals, organizational structure, processes, and policies to build and run a world-class IT organization.

Brand Your Department

Just as a company has a mission, a vision, and a set of goals, individual departments should create their own maxims to articulate how they fit into the overall picture. The mission for an IT department should describe why it is exists. Here is an example:

> The mission of Information Technology is to deliver value by providing innovative, cost-effective technology and services that are strategically aligned with business goals and objectives.

An IT department's vision is a statement of what it wants to be. It goes something like this:

> Our vision is that IT capabilities are a core competitive strength for the company.

Finally, IT goals specify how the department will enable the business through the use of technology. The following seven steps, which form the outline of this book, can be used as the principal goals for an IT department:

1. **Partner.** Establish strong relationships with internal and external stakeholders to create long-term competitive advantage.
2. **Organize.** Define the organizational structure and processes needed to run IT effectively and efficiently so that it delivers value-added products and services, seeks continuous improvement, and is prepared to adapt to business change.
3. **Innovate.** Build cost-effective and high-performance technology products and services that deliver value and are strategically aligned with business goals and objectives.
4. **Deliver.** Implement products and services to improve bottom-line performance for your company.

5. **Support.** Provide superior service to maximize the return on investment in business technology.
6. **Protect.** Manage and minimize risks so that your company can continue to operate effectively and protect its reputation.
7. **Grow.** Attract, motivate, and retain a talented team that works toward a common vision and mission.

Define an IT Organizational Model

CIOs often debate the merits of a federated IT organization over a centralized IT organization—or any other IT model du jour. Whether centralized or federated, however, most IT organizations are structured to support vertical business units or functions. IT resources and budgets in these traditional IT organizations are focused on the projects and service activities that address the discrete business activities. The problem with these traditional IT organizational structures, however, is they often fail to integrate the process to maximize business value.

In the traditional IT organization, projects are scoped and implemented without fully recognizing the core business processes that span business units or functions. With an enterprise view, organizations lose the opportunity to implement the most effective solutions. The narrow focus on individual IT projects, applications, and local business-unit needs results in an application knowledge of vertical business processes. In this environment, the strategic contribution that IT could make through service-oriented architecture (SOA) and enterprise integration is drastically reduced. In order to capitalize on the opportunities of SOA and enterprise integration, IT organizations must shift their focus to interrelated business processes and services.[1]

Table 2.1 depicts a federated organizational structure. The federated IT organization is the most commonly found structure in large IT shops.

In a federated structure, IT has a hybrid structure of business unit IT roles and a centralized shared service structure. In a federated organization, you centralize services such as networks, databases, and enterprise applications. The services you decentralize are business unit–specific applications and associated relationship management.

Table 2.1 Traditional Federated IT Organizational Structure

Function	Business Unit 1	Business Unit 2
Relationship management	Functional relationship managers	Functional relationship managers
Application development	Application development	Application development
	Functional relationship managers	
	Application development	
Shared services	Infrastructure	
	Program management office	

In the federated structure, there is no enterprise architecture and systems integration (EASI) function. If this does exist, it is generally regulated to serve an individual business function or business unit.

Finally, the relationship managers are focused on individual functions, such as sales, marketing, or accounting, in a traditional model. They generally lack a holistic view of the interrelated processes that make up customer relationship management (CRM), enterprise resource planning, or supply chain management.

In a service-oriented federated IT structure, depicted in Table 2.2, the EASI function is added at the shared services layer.

The responsibilities of the relationship managers are broadened to include multiple functions. For instance, instead of certain managers focusing on just sales or marketing, they would now own all of the functions related to CRM. They become process relationship managers (PRMs) tasked with designing and delivering an end-to-end

Table 2.2 Service-Oriented Federated IT Organizational Structure

Function	Business Unit 1	Business Unit 2
Relationship management	Process relationship managers	Process relationship managers
Application development	Application development	Application development
	Process relationship managers	
	Application development	
Shared services	Enterprise architecture and systems integration	
	Infrastructure	
	Program management office	

Table 2.3   Service-Oriented Centralized IT Organizational Structure

Function	Business Units
Function shared services	Process relationship managers Application development Enterprise architecture and systems integration Infrastructure Program management office

business-process vision. The change in responsibilities allows them to recognize the horizontal nature of the business processes.

In this example, everything the CRM team works on affects the customer's experience with the company's products and services. The PRM is in the best position to relay service-oriented business requirements to the EASI team. For instance, a PRM can collaborate with the EASI team to design a service ensuring that new customer data is available not only to the sales system but also to the marketing and customer-service systems.

In the service-oriented centralized IT organizational structure, shown in Table 2.3, the business unit–specific application development and relationship management functions are eliminated in favor of a more command-and-control structure. In this structure, all systems and budgets reside at the shared service level. While CIOs may gain greater cost control and production efficiency with this structure, they risk losing connectivity to the business.

It's clear that IT organizations are undergoing a significant shift brought about by the economic downturn, globalization, cloud computing, mobilization, and consumer technology. CIOs need an organizational structure and governance framework that is flexible and adaptive to the changing landscape. The right structure will help them to effectively partner with their business peers and deliver value-added products and services.

Define a Project Methodology

Similar to the governance framework needed to partner with the business, a set of processes and forums within IT is also necessary to ensure that your team members partner with one another to execute projects on time and within budget. For this reason, I am outlining several processes and meeting forums to help you effectively manage your project.

> A popular and effective practice is to create a variety of classifications to distinguish projects of different shapes and sizes so they can be managed appropriately.

Let's start by defining a project methodology. There are many off-the-shelf methodology frameworks an IT organization can adapt, such as the rational unified process or the agile unified process. Typically, however, most organizations start out with a standard methodology and then customize it to their liking. What is important is to have one that fits the organizational culture. Without having a common methodology, you invite chaos when every project manager uses his or her own methodology—or none at all—to manage projects.

All projects aren't created equal. A popular and effective practice is to create a variety of classifications to distinguish projects of different shapes and sizes so they can be managed appropriately within your portfolio. The following is an example of project classification:

Major Project
- Total effort is estimated to be greater than four person-months—that is, one person is dedicated to the project for four months or two people are dedicated to it for two months.
- Involves a significant investment of capital funds.
- Includes deployments of large or multiple systems affecting a large number of users.

Medium Project
- Total effort is estimated to be two to four person-months.
- Involves a moderate investment of capital funds.
- Involves significant features to systems or deployments of small systems.

Minor Project

- Total effort is estimated to be one to two person-months.
- Involves a minor investment of capital funds, if any.
- Involves a very limited number of new features to systems.

Depending on your software-release management strategy, you can treat releases as projects. The classification of a release project will depend on the frequency and size of the releases. A common project methodology and classification model will create discipline within your department and help you achieve anticipated business results.

Manage the Software Selection Process

Enterprise systems promise operational improvements that drive significant value in companies. Successful implementations have shown that promise to be achievable if the right solution is selected. Gartner Group, a large technology research firm, notes that half of enterprise system implementations fail to produce a positive return on investment in the first five years. Success begins with effectively managing the software evaluation process.

Step 1: Project Team

The initial step in the software selection process is to identify a project team. This assumes the project has already been approved and funded through the governance process that we will discuss in the next chapter.

Step 2: Requirements

Software evaluations begin with having well-documented business requirements. Once you receive written requirements from your business partners, it's time to conduct a workshop to refine detailed business requirements and identify the primary functional, technical, and vendor-related evaluation criteria.

Step 3: Assessment Model

Next, develop an assessment model based on the requirements. This model comes in many forms, but generally it consists of a list of requirements along with a weighing of importance (on a scale of 1 to 10) and a place for participants involved in the evaluation to record a score for each vendor.

Step 4: Software Vendor Research

Now it is time to identify your vendor options. This step begins with identifying a list of applicable vendors and then narrowing them down through research to identify the ones that you wish to involve in the formal evaluation process.

Step 5: Request for Proposal

The request for proposal (RFP) is a formal document that you send to the vendors requesting that they provide information on how their products and services can satisfy your business requirements. As you prepare material to send to potential software suppliers, you need to remember that the parties involved in the RFP process (your organization and the potential software supplier) have very different objectives in this process.

Your objective is to get meaningful information about various potential software suppliers that will help you to narrow the field to a manageable level. The objective of the software supplier, however, is merely to make it to the next step in your software selection process. As a result, most software suppliers will respond to an RFP with a (generally) voluminous boilerplate response document filled with largely useless information and embellishments. You will find yourself digging through this information in order to extract the information in which you are interested.

Step 6: Vendor Demonstrations

Once you have received the RFPs and you have narrowed down your list to three vendors, it is time to invite the vendors in for a demonstration. A good practice is to provide the vendors with a script that outlines what you are looking for them to provide you with during the demonstration. This allows you to learn how they will fit

---

Five Key Elements in an RFP

1. Definition of why you are seeking new software (i.e., your buying criteria).
2. Description of your business, transaction volumes, user count, and so on.
3. Clear definition of what information you are seeking from the suppliers.
4. Quantitative (rather than qualitative) evaluation criteria.
5. Definition of how the process will work and the time frames involved.

---

your requirements. Schedule time with your staff members so that they need to be available only for their areas of interest and responsibility. This helps you to compare the vendors equally.

Provide the demo attendees with the assessment model so they can rank the functionality and other offerings that you are evaluating.

After you have collected and tabulated the assessments and other information you need to make a final decision, meet with the project team to review the materials and discuss the pros and cons. If you encourage the project team members to collaborate and gain consensus, they will have more ownership of the final decision and be supportive of the vendor and the project.

Step 7: Technology Contracts

Once you have decided on the vendor you want to do business with, it's time to develop a contract. Since IT organizations typically deal with many technology contracts, it is a good idea to build some best practices to be used when outsourcing to service providers or acquiring new technologies.

I asked Susan Miller, the CIO of a major sports franchise, how she engages her technology partners so she can create effective relationships. This is what she told me:

> Developing contracts and relationships that are win-win is really the key to success with technology partnerships. Being that we are a popular sports

franchise, a lot of vendors want to hang out with us and talk about sports. It's not unusual for us to get phone calls from the leaders from the largest technology firms. While it's great to have that level of access and interest, we need to use it appropriately.

Having worked at IBM on the sales side for many years, I have learned a great deal about how to ink favorable deals and build long-lasting partnerships. For example, when I am working on a new deal with a sales representative, I always ask them how they are compensated. I am not interested in what they make, just the components that make up their compensation package, so I can understand what motivates them.

For instance, are they compensated based on a percent of gross revenue or profit? Are they paid based on my level of satisfaction with the deal? I also ask how their manager is compensated. Of course, I often get a surprised look from the sales representative when I ask these questions, so I usually begin by explaining how my project team members are compensated. I tell them, for example, that my staff will get paid a better bonus if the project is successful. This dialogue is helpful in understanding what makes people tick. I use the same approach when building partnerships with employees.

Here are Susan's tips on creating effective contracts:

Whenever you have to refer back to a contract to verify the terms of the deal, you are probably in trouble. It usually means you are not satisfied with the product or service. Good contracts are about setting the right expectations up front. So if you are feeling that you are not getting what you want out of the relationship, it is either because you didn't set the right expectations up front or the vendor is not delivering on their promise.

Either way, you are in a bad place regardless of what is written in the contract. The service level agreements have to be written in a way that is easily understood by all parties. When I worked at IBM, I drove our lawyers crazy because I wanted to put the contracts in plain English and avoid the legal mumbo jumbo.

By managing the software evaluation process through a series of logical steps, you can quickly and effectively evaluate and select an enterprise system software and technology partner that is right for your business.

Maintain a Portfolio of Products and Services

During economic turbulence, portfolio management becomes increasingly important as companies are forced to do more with less. Project portfolio management (PPM) can help you identify, categorize, and prioritize projects in relation to the business strategies and objectives across your organization. PPM helps you focus on the right projects when funding is limited, while project management can help you execute activities efficiently and effectively.

> Project portfolio management (PPM) can help you identify, categorize, and prioritize projects in relation to the business strategies and objectives across your organization.

Portfolio management enables decision makers to align their portfolios with enterprise strategy and balance risk and return. Just as personal investment portfolios are reweighted as personal goals change, IT portfolios are also reweighted as conditions change.[2]

One approach to IT portfolio analysis lists four IT asset classes, each supporting a different management objective:

1. Strategic (to gain a competitive advantage)
2. Informational (to provide information)
3. Transactional (to provide transactions and cut costs)
4. Infrastructure (to provide shared services and integration)

Classifying the enterprise's annual investments into these four categories facilitates strategic analysis and raises questions about specific decisions. For example, in an economic downturn, do we really want to allocate 40 percent of this year's IT investments to the high-risk, high-return asset class? Instead, should we reweight the portfolio toward the low-risk, solid-return, transactional-investment asset class? Alternatively, can we afford to have another year of low infrastructure investment?[3]

I am sure you remember the Chinese proverb that "a picture is worth a thousand words." In the case of PPM, CIOs can use IT

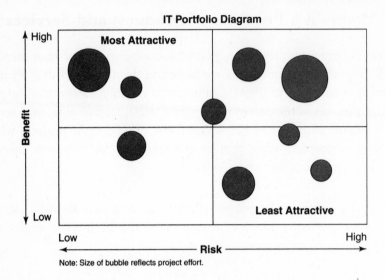

Figure 2.1   IT Portfolio Diagram

portfolio diagrams to illustrate projects according to asset classes. See Figure 2.1 for an example.

PPM is not separate from the governance framework we already discussed. In fact, PPM complements it by providing you with a companywide view of technology investments. As the governance bodies meet to identify and prioritize projects within their function (e.g., sales, marketing, or finance), portfolio management practices help you consolidate the information into a database for reporting and analysis. Individual projects across functional areas invariably compete for the same IT resources, so having reports that roll up estimated funding, resource, and time requirements can give you a great view of the pressure points.

Once you have categorized the projects into the four IT asset classes, you can assess the projects based on three dimensions:

1. **Benefit proposition.** What is the return on the investment?
2. **Risk.** What is the likelihood of completing the project on time and within budget? Do you have the funding and skilled resources? Is the project introducing new technologies, or is it leveraging the existing architecture?

3. **Effort.** What is the expected level of resources and time required to complete the project?

With this information, you can evaluate the mix of projects across the dimensions, such as risk and value, and use scenario planning to help you decide which projects make the most sense to tackle.

It is a best practice to establish a portfolio management committee (PMC) within IT to monitor and measure progress with each of the projects in the portfolio. The PMC is typically made up of IT leaders representing each of the major functions: relationship management, infrastructure, application development, EASI, and the program management office. The frequency of the meetings greatly depends on the number of projects or major issues. The PMC reviews progress toward each of the projects. This is achieved by requiring that the project managers present to the committee each time they reach a milestone and are seeking approval to go on to the next phase of the project (e.g., design, develop, or test).

I recently met with David Colville, the CIO of Nestlé Waters North America (NWNA). NWNA bottles and distributes 15 well-known bottled-water brands. Most of these are sold regionally and are leaders in their distribution areas. NWNA's North American brand, Nestlé Pure Life, is sold throughout the United States and Canada. Nonsparkling water represents more than 90 percent of sales.

I asked David how he manages his portfolio of products and services at NWNA. This is what he told me:

> Portfolio management is very complex in a global company where individual countries are dependent upon shared service entities for technology products and services. It requires careful partnering and collaboration with local, regional, and global program management offices to communicate business requirements and then manage changes to our existing portfolio.
>
> The same concept can be applied to a domestic business with many operating units. While a disadvantage of the shared service structure may be slower time to market in some cases, we have enjoyed an overall lower cost of ownership with our shared technologies. For instance, a particular innovation developed in one country can be reused throughout many countries in a global company. Also, our portfolio management process is helping us to focus on the right investments.

PPM Software

There are plenty of commercially available software products that can undoubtedly help you get started with PPM. However, if you are at level-one maturity with PPM, don't expect to be achieving level five just because you install an expensive piece of software. You first need to implement a governance process so you can capture the data points required to use PPM software. Also, you need to be sure that you have executive sponsorship and the organization is prepared to embrace the effort.

The choice of tool is not as important as delivering the discipline required for PPM. The level of discipline that you can achieve depends on your company's culture and appetite for a structured approach to project assessments. For instance, a company that produces commercial software will typically have an easier time convincing its staff to capture time spent on each activity in a PPM system than a company that is not in the software business will.

Understand Your Capacity

Choosing and monitoring the right applications and projects does little good without people with the proper skills to implement and maintain them. Resource management is critical to the concept of an IT governance process that understands people and the intellectual capital they possess as vital corporate assets. The good news is that tools and processes are available that provide in-depth employee information to carefully monitor resource assignments in terms of complete visibility into the project portfolio, alignment with key strategic goals, risks associated with leaving or being shifted to another assignment, costs and benefits, and portfolio balance.[4]

First, you need a clear view of the existing and future projects that the PPM process has already prioritized. Second, you need to step back and view the entire workforce, with each person clearly delineated within the system by his or her skill sets and levels of expertise. Once that is done, conduct a utilization or capacity analysis of both current and future demand that reveals surpluses and gaps by business unit, manager, or location. Performing what-if scenarios can also help forecast resource availability for the weeks and months ahead. The level of analysis you are able to perform on a portfolio will depend on the amount of data you are able to collect from your team on a routine basis.

This approach is enhanced by preliminarily allocating people to both existing and future projects in ways visible to all appropriate managers. This allows project managers to proactively negotiate project assignments.

Create IT Policies

IT policies are designed to help you support value delivery while managing significant risks, encouraging cooperation, and promoting compliance. A policy is a documented set of basic principles and associated guidelines, formulated and enforced by the governing body of an organization. In the case of IT policies, the policies are written by IT management and generally approved by an overarching policy committee within an organization.

Here is a sample list of policies worth considering for your department:

- Network access
- E-mail use
- Passwords
- Backups
- Technical issue reporting
- Remote access
- Guest access
- Wireless access
- Social media
- Confidential data
- Mobile device
- Data retention

These policies should include the purpose, roles and responsibilities, exception process, compliance expectations, procedures, and references to related policies and procedures.

Interesting to note is that while IT departments often create a lot of policies for company employees to follow, the IT employees themselves are not always as familiar with the policies as they should be. Periodically reviewing one of the policies at each management meeting, or even each full staff meeting, is a good way to build awareness. After all, you and your team need to set a good example for all employees to follow. You will be surprised at what you and your staff actually learns from reviewing the policies. It is also quite common to find opportunities for improving policies through this process.

Manage the Technology Partners

In an effort to ensure that the products and services provided by your technology partners meet your business requirements and minimize risks, an effective partner relationship-management program should be developed and adopted. Successful IT partnerships are established and fostered by clearly defining the roles, responsibilities, and expectations between the parties. I call these people *partners* rather than *vendors* or *suppliers* because I consider them extensions of my own team.

A partner relationship-management program helps define the processes, the guiding principles, and even a system for creating and maintaining effective relationships with your suppliers.

First, create a document that outlines the scope and approach of the program. The major components of such a program include contract management and technology partner summits. The following is an overview of these components.

Contract Management

An IT department typically manages relationships with dozens—in some cases, hundreds—of technology firms. Managing the contracts with these firms can become quite burdensome if you don't take the time to develop efficient contract-management practices. Of course, there are plenty of software choices available to help you get started.

Start with documenting how you will centralize the storage of the actual contracts so you can easily locate these crucial documents when you need them. Consider setting automated alerts for important contract dates. Here are the data elements you generally find in a contract-management system (CMS):

- Partner name
- Responsible manager
- Partner type (software, equipment, or service)
- License agreement
- License agreement's expiration date
- Maintenance agreement
- Maintenance agreement's expiration date
- Nonsolicitation agreement
- Nonsolicitation agreement's expiration date
- Nondisclosure
- Statement of work
- Termination date
- Reason for termination
- Termination approval

Once you have created a repository for your contracts, create reports and alerts to help you keep on top of expiration dates. The key is being aware that a contract is about to expire months in advance so you have the opportunity to negotiate a renewal when you are in a position of strength.

A CMS also helps you reduce the risk of data loss when an employee who is managing one or more contracts suddenly leaves your company. You can simply run a report listing the contracts that the employee was managing and reassign responsibility.

Technology Partner Summits

According to a research study conducted by McKinsey & Company, although a majority of technology executives want to have stronger relationships with their IT suppliers, they often act in ways that undermine that goal. In fact, many corporate customers lose out on the potential benefit of a closer relationship by engaging in value-destroying or inconsistent behavior (e.g., too much emphasis on costs) when they interact with vendors.[5]

McKinsey interviewed IT executives at 23 companies, representing a wide range of industries, to learn about technology-purchasing patterns. Although 20 percent of the executives they interviewed regard costs, not added value, as the top priority, 70 percent said they want to move away from pure transactional relationships by establishing stronger partnerships with a smaller number of preferred IT suppliers.

According to a research study conducted by McKinsey & Company, although a majority of technology executives want to have stronger relationships with their IT suppliers, they often act in ways that undermine that goal.

These relationship-seeking customers want vendors who better understand their specific technical environment, offer specific ongoing advice, help them manage aggressive technology upgrade-and-innovation cycles, and provide solutions for their most pressing business problems.

One way to foster and nurture relationships with your partners is to hold partner summits. The significance of the relationship with a partner will influence the frequency of the summits. Generally speaking, however, summits are conducted on a semiannual or an annual basis. Summits are an opportunity to review service measurements, share technical road maps between organizations, review the financials of the partner to ensure they are financially sound, review satisfaction levels with products and services, and discuss any major issues or business opportunities. Also, having these meetings in person will offer you the opportunity to have the partner present to your staff.

Alan Matula, the CIO of Royal Dutch Shell, is getting vendors to abide by new rules for their behavior when delivering technology, collaborating on business problems and, as the collective gels, opening up research and development work. In a given year, Shell awards ecosystem suppliers between $1.8 billion and $2 billion, or about half of its annual IT budget of approximately $3.6 billion. Spending so much with so few vendors buys Shell access to those vendors' best talent and lets it influence their product features and larger research efforts, says Boris Van Der Weele, the supplier manager of Shell's consulting providers, such as Accenture, Deloitte, and McKinsey.

All 11 ecosystem vendors meet with Shell every quarter, in person and through telepresence and Web conferencing, to update Shell's IT governance committee on significant projects. Every month, Matula holds his "one pager," a meeting where his supplier managers update him on any problems and on what's going on with each ecosystem supplier's work, in a summary kept to one printed page. Once a year, one of the vendors hosts fellow ecosystem members to discuss their work at Shell. Microsoft hosted in 2009, and SAP (a market leader in enterprise application software) hosted in 2010.[6]

> "I suppose if I were a government employee in charge of technology contracts, I would probably be fired because I don't have an interest in bidding out work to dozens of suppliers."
> —John Hinkle, CIO, Take-Two Interactive Inc.

Matula's strategy doesn't apply only to megasized companies such as Royal Dutch Shell. John Hinkle, the CIO of Take-Two Interactive Inc., also prefers to work with a handful of strategic partners:

> *I try to form strong relationships with a small number of partners and run 90 percent of my business through them. I suppose if I were a government employee in charge of technology contracts, I would probably be fired because I don't have an interest in bidding out work to dozens of suppliers. It's not that my preferred suppliers always win the business. Their products and services have to meet my requirements, but I do try to limit the number of suppliers that I do business with so I can maximize the value out of the relationships.*

I recently sat down with Ken Murdoch, the CIO of Save the Children, the leading independent organization creating lasting change in the lives of children in need in the United States and around the world. Save the Children works with other organizations, governments, nonprofits, and a variety of local partners while maintaining its own independence without a political agenda or a religious orientation.

I had the pleasure of working with Ken at Pepsi-Cola in the 1990s, and I always admired his professionalism, work ethic, and character. It's difficult not to be impressed by his altruism and passion for charity. To get a sense of the other side of the spectrum, I asked Ken how he engages his technology partners, given that he has a significantly smaller budget than the CIOs I just mentioned. This is what he shared with me:

> Our technology partners need to be just that—partners. We do not have deep pockets for major investments. Vendors need to work with us in a spirit of using their technology "for good," and the value they get is to have our brand on their website as a representation of their philanthropic spirit, core values, and beliefs. The benefits we receive are in what is called "in-kind" donations, where we can put their technology to use and help us to be competitive and drive lasting and positive change for children around the world.

Brian R. Lurie, the senior vice president and CIO of Teleflex, has a win-win philosophy when it comes to technology partnerships:

> When I am in trouble, I want to know I have a vendor out there who wants to help me, not because they have to, but because they are going to feel really bad if they don't. I build strong relationships with my vendors so that they would be embarrassed not to be there when I need their help. In exchange, I make sure my vendors get my business if they deserve it.
>
> It takes a lot of time to foster a personal relationship with a vendor. It involves a lot of communication, even when things are working well. We like to invite vendors to participate on steering committees for major projects, so they are invested in the project and have skin in the game. A vendor doesn't want to come to a steering committee and find out it was their piece that was broken.

Benchmark IT

Industry research organizations, such as Gartner Group and Forrester, provide benchmarking data for many industries. As good as they are—and they are very good—they don't cover all industries, company sizes, or geographies, and they don't always provide answers to the specific questions you may have about your competitors. Also, they can be expensive for small or midmarket companies.

If you are interested in benchmarking IT at your company and don't have the budget for third-party research data, why not create your own survey and target the companies you're interested in? Even if you happen to lead a very large organization and have the budget for research data, a customized approach can help you pinpoint the information you are seeking.

I asked Greg Fell, the CIO of Terex Corporation, how he gathers benchmarking data from other IT shops. Here is his reply:

> While I use IT industry research from firms such as Gartner Group, I prefer the face-to-face discussions with my CIO peers. While at Ford Motor Company, I spearheaded an annual benchmarking study with companies such as Boeing, Intel, and British Petroleum. I found it to be useful to meet with companies of similar size and scale. The methods we would use to address issues with tens of thousands of desktops would be markedly different from a company that is managing a few hundred desktops.

Save the Children's Murdoch relies on surveys for benchmarking data:

> We use scorecards or dashboards for major projects monthly, and we have quarterly scorecards for other IT work. We annually benchmark against other NGOs [non-governmental organizations] to see where we match up. Our annual customer-satisfaction surveys measure internal satisfaction and the success of our work. Our annual NGO benchmark surveys measure if we are achieving goals and meeting or beating categorical leading indicators like overall budget versus user base, geographical reach of user base, overall revenues, and staff size to user base.

If you have been in your role or industry for a few years, you are likely to have established contacts with your peers at other companies. I have found the community of CIOs to be generally open and collaborative and willing to share information about its operations.

Here are five tips for creating an effective and useful IT benchmarking survey:

1. **Keep it short.** If you ask 50 questions, no one is going to respond. Would you want to respond? Ask questions that will generate meaningful information for you and the survey respondents. For instance, asking what business application software the recipients are using to support their accounting processes isn't very helpful on its own. Consider asking follow-up questions such as:

   • Is it your primary software for this process? (They may be using multiple systems.)

- What percentage of targeted users in the company are using the software?
- What is the user satisfaction level for the software?

2. **Make it collaborative.** Before sending out the survey, take time to ask your peers what questions they would like to have included in the survey. Getting your peers involved in the design of the survey usually earns you more responses.

3. **Review the results with the respondents.** Consider conducting a teleconference or an in-person meeting after the survey with the respondents to discuss the results. In-person meetings are more effective because they allow you an opportunity to build relationships and discuss related topics that were not part of the survey. CIOs are generally generous with sharing information and enjoy the face-to-face discussions to collaborate.

4. **In addition to doing traditional IT benchmarking, consider helping your company perform competitive benchmarking by researching how other companies in your industry are using technology.** While David Kaufman, the CIO at Aramark Corporation, performs the requisite IT benchmarking studies, such as IT spending as a percentage of revenue, he prefers to focus on *competitive* benchmarking—not on dollars spent but on areas that are competitive differentiators in the marketplace. As David describes it:

> To be viewed as a partner to the business, it's important for CIOs to learn how competitors are leveraging technology to grow the business. For example, I recently learned that a competitor of our corrections business is selling prepaid calling cards so that prison inmates can make phone calls to their loved ones. This is the type of competitive analysis that I incorporate in my presentations to the strategic committee when proposing new initiatives. This helps the committee understand if my proposal is helping the company catch up to a competitor or whether it will offer the company a competitive differentiator.

5. **Share the results with your staff, business partners, and management.** Incorporate results into your overall IT communication program and include it in communications to your

staff, users, and management. Share the information regardless of whether it's favorable or unfavorable to your department. If you omit or disguise facts to make the results appear to be more favorable to your department, you are missing the point of the exercise. It is expected that a competitor will be doing some things better than you, and the benchmarking is a great way to get your team motivated and focused on continuous improvement. Also, misrepresenting the data will ultimately result in you losing credibility and trust within your company.

Consider conducting the survey on an annual basis so you can identify trends in budgets, standards, technology initiatives, and priorities. A sample benchmarking survey is available on the companion website.

The community of CIOs is generally open and collaborative and willing to share information about its operations.

Top Plays

- CIOs need to adopt an organizational structure to support changing business paradigms brought on by the economic downturn, globalization, cloud computing, mobilization, and consumerization of technology.
- A common project methodology and classification model creates order and discipline for projects and helps you achieve anticipated results.
- Success begins with effective management of technology partners.
- PPM can help you identify, categorize, and prioritize projects in relation to the business strategies and objectives across your organization.

(continued)

- A partner relationship-management program helps define the processes, guiding principles, and even system for creating and maintaining effective relationships with your suppliers.
- Conduct your own IT benchmarking to gather the information you are seeking and save dollars.

Notes

1. TIBCO Software, *TIBCO Service-Oriented IT Organizational Structure Best Practices: An Introduction*, (Palo Alto, CA: privately printed, 2005), 2–3.

2. Peter Weill and Jeanne W. Ross, *IT Governance: How Top Performers Manage IT Decision Rights for Superior Results* (Boston: Harvard Business School Publishing, 2004), 46.

3. *Ibid.*, 47.

4. Oracle, *Positioning the CIO as a Powerful Business Partner with IT Portfolio Governance* (Redwood Shores, CA: privately printed, 2010), 7–8.

5. Baljit Dail and Andy West, "Building Stronger IT Vendor Relationships," *McKinsey & Company Newsletter* (NJ), Spring 2005.

6. Kim S. Nash, "CIOs Forge Vendor Collectives to Extract Business Benefits," *CIO*, November 28, 2011.

Chapter 3

Step 3: Innovate

Innovation distinguishes between a leader and a follower.

—*Steve Jobs*

Innovate: Build cost-effective and high-performance IT products and services that deliver value and are strategically aligned with business goals and objectives.

Where does innovation come from? Some ideas come from your business partners, other ideas come from your customers and suppliers, and some of the best ideas come from your IT staff. Innovations come in many shapes and sizes. Some are incremental improvements that improve operational efficiencies or create a small advantage over competitors. Other innovations are more radical and create new business opportunities. In either case, you need a process to capture, evaluate, and act on the ideas. This chapter describes a comprehensive but practical method to tap into your company's rising reservoir of new, undeveloped, and untried methods to solve real business problems.

Turn Ideas into Action

To capitalize on innovation in a competitive global economy, CIOs must solve today's problems yesterday by seizing opportunities to leverage emerging technologies. Innovation expert Arthur VanGundy noted that innovation has hit the corporate world with a force unknown in previous generations of business trends; however, profit-driven organizations have not been alone. Globalization of technology, media, cultures, commerce, and the new economy has created a momentum to forge new directions with customers and clients. Managers in profit, nonprofit, government, military, and educational institutions all now face the unenviable task of innovating like never before. The call has gone out for new ideas, fresh perspectives, and unique approaches to solving old problems. In addition to the need for institutionalizing innovation processes, all organizations must confront the realities of how to define the challenges they face.[1]

> To capitalize on innovation in a competitive global economy, CIOs must solve today's problems yesterday by seizing opportunities to leverage emerging technologies.

IT is in a unique position to harness ideas from all over the organization and then synthesize those ideas into actionable projects. You can use technology to make previously impractical thoughts a reality. However, not all ideas are good ones, so you will need a well-thought-out process to review potential innovations and decide which ones are truly aligned with the company's vision and goals and will produce positive business outcomes.

Create a Governance Framework

Chapter 1 described the importance of helping the business establish priorities by forming and actively participating in committees. Since innovation is highly dependent on structured and efficient committees, let's delve a bit deeper into how to create a governance framework.

Renowned research scientists Peter Weill and Jeanne W. Ross described IT governance as specifying the decision rights and account-ability framework to encourage desirable behavior in using IT. IT governance reflects broader governance principles while focusing on the management and use of IT to achieve corporate performance goals. Effective IT governance encourages and leverages the ingenuity of the enterprise's people in IT usage and ensures compliance with the enterprise's overall vision and values.[2]

Governance is the responsibility of executives and consists of the leadership, organizational structures, and processes that ensure that the company's IT sustains and extends the organization's strategies and objectives. For IT to be successful in innovating and delivering according to business requirements, management must institute a framework designed to manage the collaboration between IT and the rest of the business. Think of governance less as a method to enforce IT policies and more as a way to generate innovative ideas to improve products and services.

According to control objectives for information and related tech-nology (which goes by the acronym COBIT), an IT governance framework, strategic alignment focuses on ensuring the linkage of busi-ness and IT plans; on defining, maintaining, and validating the IT value proposition; and on aligning IT operations with enterprise operations. COBIT does an excellent job of defining what a partnership looks like when it's achieved. This section will describe techniques to help you get started, however. The following is a list of committees that make up a typical governance framework:

- **Steering committee.** An overarching body of executives is responsible for overseeing the development and implementation of standardized policies, processes, and systems throughout a com-pany. Simply put, governance and the effective application of a governance framework are the responsibilities of executive man-agement. The steering committee provides oversight to ensure that the business policies, processes, and IT investments are aligned with business needs.

- **Process leadership committees (PLCs).** These committees review and gain consensus and priorities on changes to business policies, procedures, processes, and systems and validate that all global and regional requirements are addressed.
- **System user groups (SUGs).** These groups are a trusted source for experience-driven education and peer networking and serve as the collective influential voice of users to shape the future of a company's business software. Together, the various SUGs form a year-round ecosystem of intellectual capital, create knowledge-sharing opportunities, and serve as a forum to influence software design. These groups identify requirements for software changes and set priorities.
- **Release management committee.** This group schedules the development and delivery of system innovations and the supporting policies, procedures, and processes that have been approved by the aforementioned committees.

Let's examine the following factors that will help you administer the governing bodies: membership, membership terms, proxies, chairperson duties, frequency of meetings, reviews of submitted business requests, and summits.

Membership

When you are establishing membership for your governance committees, it is essential that you balance the committees with representatives from each of the business units using the enterprise processes and systems. If most of the members are from corporate management, you will alienate the rest of the business and risk the governance committees' losing their objectivity.

Membership Terms

You can choose to either have term limits or not. The advantage of not having term limits is that you have a consistency of knowledge and experience on your committees. The disadvantage is that you lose the benefit of fresh ideas. If you choose to not impose term limits, then the chairperson should at least reconfirm the membership of each of the members each year with the executive team. The chairperson should also nominate new members in situations where a current member is no longer able to perform their duties.

Think of governance less as a method to enforce IT policies and more as a way to generate innovative ideas to improve products and services.

Proxies

Voting should be done by the members attending each meeting and noted in the official minutes. The items to be voted on by the committee should be outlined in the agenda sent out by the chairperson. A good practice is to require a quorum of two-thirds of the members, including designated alternates, to initiate the approval of any item. A rejected item may be resubmitted to the committee after a certain period—twelve months works well in many organizations.

I once had a business-unit president tell me he didn't think the governance process was working because he was not being made aware of proposed changes to the business processes before the changes were approved. In essence, he was being surprised by the changes. The problem was that the employees he assigned to the PLCs to represent his business unit were not giving him and his leadership team an opportunity to weigh in on the change proposals before the voting took place. The framework should state that each PLC member is responsible for reviewing the change proposals with his or her respective leadership team for awareness and approval prior to a vote.

Furthermore, the framework should give the steering committee an opportunity to oppose a change proposal even if the PLC approved it. A best practice is to give the steering committee a ratification period of 10 days to comment on the proposal. Only those proposals that are controversial (e.g., more than one steering committee member does not agree with the proposal) should be sent to the steering committee for discussion and final approval. Otherwise, silence regarding the proposal is understood as acceptance.

The success of governance comes down to the quality of the people who are assigned to represent the business and how well they communicate with the leadership team. While you may have smart people on the committees, some may have poor communication skills and cause issues, such as the one I just described. Conversely, just because someone happens to be a great communicator—or happens to have some extra time—doesn't mean that he or she is qualified to represent the business on a governance body.

You want to avoid having senior-level executives who feel the process is not working simply because unqualified people are assigned to the committees or the people who are assigned do not have good communication skills. You have to address issues as quickly as possible to ensure a successful governance program.

Chairperson Duties

The following is a list of the typical responsibilities of a chairperson:

- Setting the agenda.
- Scheduling the meetings and arranging facilities.
- Facilitating each meeting.
- Communicating change requests for discussion and voting.
- Keeping employees aware of the status of their change requests.
- Monitoring the status of issues and action items addressed by the committee.
- Distributing the required materials.
- Recording and distributing the meeting minutes within five business days after the meeting.
- Ensuring that the membership is updated on a timely basis.
- Inviting guest participants.
- Attending peer committee meetings as a guest, as appropriate, to share and gain approval on changes that may have cross-functional effects.
- Communicating proposed changes to the steering committee for awareness and for the opportunity for the steering sommittee to oppose a change request.

Frequency of Meetings

It's reasonable to expect the committees to meet at least four times per calendar year (once per quarter). You may want to allow the committees to meet fewer than four times if there are no agenda items that warrant a meeting. Conversely, a committee may have additional meetings to address time-sensitive issues, such as the technology required to support a national marketing campaign. Given the scrutiny on spending in a down economy coupled with advances in communications capabilities, the chairperson should be encouraged to conduct the meetings by video conference, webinar, or teleconference.

A sample governance framework template is available on the companion website.

Reviews of Submitted Business Requests

To achieve effective governance, executives expect controls to be implemented by operational managers within the defined control framework for all of the functions we discussed. This collaboration and alignment is essential for you to deliver innovation that streamline operations and boosts your organization's competitive standing.

It's a good practice to design a business-case template for employees to use when submitting major proposals to the committees. You may also want to develop templates to support a variety of smaller requests: new system features, processes, reports, and so on. Committee members are responsible for reviewing requests and providing timely, informative reviews of the requests. In the next section, I describe best practices for developing a winning business case.

Summits

I continually discover ways to improve the framework. I am not talking about major changes, just little tweaks that usually occur on an annual basis. One example is the formation of what I refer to as a summit. I've learned that if you have tightly integrated business processes, you will find the need to bring multiple PLCs or SUGs together from time to time to address cross-functional issues.

Summits follow the same rules as governance committees but just involve more representatives. It may be a session that includes PLC members from accounting, sales, and purchasing, for instance. To keep the group to a reasonable size, the steering committee can help by nominating individuals from each of the required committees to attend and represent the areas. Sometimes the issue has such an effect on the business that some of the steering committee members themselves attend the summit to listen in on the discussion (although that tends to intimidate the members, so I generally discourage the practice).

It's important that everyone understands the ground rules for the summit. For instance, does everyone in the room (or virtual room) get a vote? Is the membership fairly representative of the organizational structure? For instance, if your company has four business regions, are all regions equally represented?

It is imperative that the chairperson respects the governance framework. For instance, I experienced a situation where a process chairman abruptly invited members of three PLCs to a teleconference to try to make a decision on a high-impact issue. There was no agenda to speak of and no business case, and not all of the members were able to make the meeting at such late notice. We ended up basically throwing a wet blanket on the meeting in favor of arranging a proper summit, but the damage was already done. The process owner had abused his power out of self-interest. I learned an important lesson: Governance is extremely powerful, and it should be used wisely and appropriately. Otherwise, you risk jeopardizing the integrity of the framework.

Governance: One Size Does Not Fit All

I have described a very formal governance framework, but some companies prefer a less structured approach. Jon Harding, the CIO of Conair Corporation, describes Conair as a fast-moving company where most priorities are established through individually held discussions with senior leaders rather than committees.

Jon explains, "The governance model really has to fit the culture of the organization. It can also differ by country in a global organization. For instance, we tend to have more structure and presentation-driven priority setting in France but rely more on individual informal discussions with senior leaders in the United States." He adds, "Even the most sophisticated governance models can be easily upended as the business changes, so it's important that CIOs are tuned into the business so they can flex their approach based on organizational priorities."

Demonstrate the Possibilities

As mentioned earlier, some of the best ideas will come from your own staff and not the actual users of the technology. A best practice is to balance a structured approach for innovation, such as the one described in this chapter, with experimentation. IT organizations should be free to perform research and development outside the governance framework. Google is probably best known for this philosophy; it offers its engineers "20 percent time" so that they're free to work on what they're really passionate about. That being said, new innovations should ultimately be presented to the governance bodies for approval.

Gary Boyd, the CIO of Windsor Health Group, believes innovation translates into competitive advantage. He is helping to change the mind-set at Windsor from merely keeping up with its competitors, to leapfrogging its competitors. "In the heavily regulated Medicare environment, technological advances are often dampened by bureaucratic approval processes," explains Gary. For the past year, he has pined for streamlining the customer enrollment process for Medicare insurance plans.

"While we have been successful in digitizing the enrollment process for some of our Medicare and insurance products using the Internet," he adds, "the Medicare supplement insurance plans require paper-based application forms that are unique to each of the 50 states. The processing of the paper-based forms is extremely costly and slow."

Recognizing the value gained by moving to online forms for the Medicare and insurance products, the company set out to work with each state's department of insurance to gain approval for online forms for the insurance plans. Of course, this process would take many months to complete, and it would force the company to continue with the expensive and slow paper-based process.

Gary had an idea for an interim solution that would help Windsor get a leg up on its competition. He partnered with Netpage, a producer of digital pen technology, and mPhasis, a software-consulting provider, to see if they could come up with a way to help sign up customers—and a pilot project was born. Using Netpage's digital pen technology, an agent records pen strokes on the application forms and then uploads the data to Windsor's backend systems to expedite the approval and fulfillment process.

"We are already seeing promising benefits in terms of reducing administrative costs and turnaround time," notes Gary. Windsor's customers are now receiving their ID cards and welcome packages much quicker than before. "Sometimes you have to burn the fields to make them fertile again," says Gary. It's clear that he and his team are bringing much-needed innovation to an industry fraught with rigid controls.

Steve Jobs was well-known for deciding what customers ultimately wanted, so he didn't think it was necessary to ask them. Walter Isaacson captured the essence of Jobs's view in his autobiography, *Steve Jobs*:

> Jobs also decided to eliminate the cursor arrow keys on the Macintosh keyboard. The only way to move the cursor was to use the mouse. It was a way of forcing old-fashioned users to adapt to point-and-click navigation, even if they didn't want to. Unlike other product developers, Jobs didn't believe the customer was always right; if they wanted to resist using the mouse, they were wrong.[3]

I asked John Hinkle, the CIO of Take-Two Interactive Software, how he and his team are helping the company with innovation. This is what he told me:

> *There are two types of innovation in our company: product innovation and process innovation. The product innovation (the games) is performed by the product development teams, which are not part of the information technology organization. Up until just a few years ago, games were created in a studio and the product development teams worked independently from the rest of the company. However, as our company grew, it was becoming a challenge to ensure that the product and marketing teams were using the final version of the marketing collateral to promote the products.*
>
> *We were also finding that money was being spent on developing new collateral when we could have just reused existing assets, such as pictures, game trailers, and advertisements. This is where process innovation came into play, and IT was ready to help. We are working to launch a collaborative platform and set of processes whereby product and marketing teams could store, access, and reuse product assets. The product and marketing teams have been very receptive to the technology and processes, and the company is eager to realize efficiencies and cost savings.*

Some companies promote Skunk Works projects to get the innovative juices flowing. At Pharmaceutical Product Development Inc., CIO Rob Petrie has set up a technology "petting zoo," composed of a rotating team of IT staffers who come from diverse backgrounds and are taken out of their regular jobs to spend six months experimenting with various technologies. Their goal is to discover ways that new technologies could be applied to deliver business results. "We always have at least five or six things in motion in the group," said Petrie. "Bringing different people through and then returning them to IT is a way to cross-pollinate ideas. It spreads innovation."[4]

We are fortunate to live in a time when technology is a driving force of business innovation. Technology is both a commodity and a competitive advantage for companies. Many breakthroughs in business have been enabled by technology. As a CIO, you have to take risks and demonstrate what is possible.

Take, for instance, Starbucks' former CIO Stephen Gillett. In early 2009, Gillett pitched the Starbucks executive council on what he called startup funding: a "series A" venture-capital investment in a new business unit called Digital Ventures. Gillett got the go-ahead, and since creating Digital Ventures, Starbucks has become a leader in mobile payments.

Gillett's digital and IT teams have also improved the company's loyalty card system, in part by developing smartphone apps that complement the loyalty cards. They created a digital network in the United States that offers free in-store Wi-Fi as well as content that customers would normally have to pay for. For making technology a much bigger part of the Starbucks customer experience while also helping the company improve its operations and processes, Gillett has earned recognition as *InformationWeek's* 2011 Chief of the Year.[5]

Think Big

It's inspiring to read stories of how CIOs moved beyond waiting for business requirements to identifying requirements and solutions. These CIOs didn't sit around and blame users for their lack of innovative ideas; they stuck out their necks and identified opportunities to leverage technology to gain competitive advantage. Also, their ideas weren't small, they were huge. That doesn't mean that suggesting incremental innovations is a bad thing, but to really stand out and make a difference in your company, you have to think big.

Successful innovation is a blend of top-down and bottom-up discovery and experimentation. Apple and Google, for instance, appear to have very different approaches to innovation, but they both have blended approaches to it. While Apple is known for giving customers what they want before they ask for it, the company is also known for displaying openness to new ideas, which is evident by its recent purchase of Siri, a voice-based personal assistant application for the iPhone. Google, known for allowing its employees to spend 20 percent of their time working on whatever projects they are interested in, has shown signs of top-down leadership since Larry Page, the cofounder, took over as the CEO in 2011.

In *Innovation to the Core: A Blueprint for Transforming the Way Your Company Innovates*, Peter Skarzynski and Rowan Gibson argued that innovation needs to become a routine practice in your organization:

> Imagine if every person in your firm came to work every day believing their ideas could influence the destiny of the company. Imagine if every corner of your organization was pulsing—at all times—with radical, rule-breaking concepts for new products, services, strategies, and businesses, providing you with a continual flow of innovations with which to delight your customers, confound your competitors, and richly reward your shareholders.

> - Imagine you could go online 24/7 and get a comprehensive, real-time window on your company's global innovation activities.
> - Imagine if every single one of your employees, at every level and in every location, had been trained in the principles, skills, and tools of innovation—greatly enhancing their ability to discover new insights, spot unexploited opportunities, and generate novel business ideas.
> - Imagine, too, that your company had a worldwide innovation infrastructure where those people could quickly find the cash, the talent, and the management support they needed to turn their ideas into market success stories.

- Simply put, imagine if the notion of building and sustaining a deep, corporate-wide capability for innovation were not just a vague aspiration but a daily reality inside your own organization.
- Now stop imagining. At some of the world's leading companies—GE, P&G, IBM, Whirlpool, Royal Dutch/Shell, CEMEX, Best Buy, W. L. Gore, and others—much of the above is already happening.

What does it take for a company to be viewed as innovative in their own industry? Being innovative doesn't always mean being the first to some up with an idea. It is a new interpretation of something. Computer timesharing has been around for a very long time, but yet cloud computing is considered a new computing paradigm.[6]

Steve Jobs once said, "We have always been shameless about stealing great ideas."[7] Leaders can learn a lot just by paying attention to what their competitors are doing. In his highly acclaimed book *Leading the Revolution*, Gary Hamel described what industry revolution is all about. Here is what he wrote:

Industry revolutionaries don't tinker at the margins; they blow up old business models and create new ones. In most companies, a call for "more innovation" is interpreted as a plea for new products or new features on old products. In this sense, most people possess a highly truncated view of innovation. They suffer from what I sometimes call the "Double Stuf Oreo" phenomenon. At Nabisco, innovation is when you stuff twice as much filling between two chocolate cookies as you used to. Don't get me wrong, Oreos are great cookies, and Double Stuf Oreos are even better, but that is not a business concept innovation—it is a linear innovation focused on a single component of the business model. Make no mistake, product innovation is still important. When, after years of trying, Clorox managed to create lemon-scented bleach, it drove the category into double-digit growth. And anyone who's shaved with Gillette's Mach III razor knows why it commands a price premium. Yet a product-based view of innovation is excessively narrow. I'm not sure that Starbucks coffee is better than what I can get in any gourmet food shop, but it's served up inside a very different business model—one that blends conviviality and theater with the java.[8]

So think big and create a culture of innovation within your company. Consider forming a Skunk Works team, or pitch a big idea to your leadership team. The worst that can happen is that your idea gets rejected. You will have more ideas. Failing is often better than not trying at all.

Develop Business Cases

A business case serves as an input into governance body meetings so that members have a clear understanding of what is being proposed so they can make informed decisions. The document is used to outline how a project will address current business concerns, the recommendations and rationale of the project, and the justification. The business case also discusses detailed project goals, performance measures, assumptions, constraints, and alternative options.

A business case contains the following sections:

1. Executive overview
2. Situation analysis
3. Recommendation and rationale
4. Alternatives analysis
5. Implementation plan
6. Approvals

Let's look at each of the sections and describe the contents for developing a comprehensive business case.

> A business case serves as an input into governance body meetings so that members have a clear understanding of what is being proposed so they can make informed decisions.

Executive Overview

The executive overview is a summary of the business case and should be written only after you have finished writing the rest of the sections. It should tell the audience why you are writing the business case: the purpose, the problem you are solving (situation analysis), what you are proposing (recommendation), why it's the right solution (rationale), and the action you are requesting from the reader.

A well-written overview should be precise and involve no more than two paragraphs. It provides the readers with the salient points to make a decision without having to read any further—unless they are interested in more information.

Situation Analysis

The situation analysis should briefly describe the business problem that the recommendation will address. This section should have an objective tone. It deals with the facts and avoids opinion.

Keep this section short. In fact, use a numbered list of the issues. Each numbered issue should begin with a strong topic sentence followed by a few sentences to further explain the problem. Readers quickly tire of reading history and tend to skip to the recommendation. This is your opportunity to convey the foundation of why you're writing the proposal. If you include too much history, the readers will skip ahead out of boredom and fail to understand the reason behind your proposal. So, keep it short by using a numbered list of issues and pithy statements that get to the heart of the issues.

Recommendation and Rationale

Begin the recommendation and rationale section with a statement of the recommendation. You can usually accomplish this in one paragraph that includes what you are proposing and a brief explanation of how it will be accomplished. Include a summary of the costs.

Next, create a numbered list of the reasons your proposal should be approved. Each numbered reason should begin with a strong topic sentence followed by a few sentences to further support the reason. Always start with the most important reason and work down to the least important reason. Include how the proposal is aligned with the company's goals and objectives.

Include a cost-benefit analysis in this section—many consider this to be the most important component of a business case. It's usually the page that readers flip to the moment they pick up a business case.

Also, include any risks and constraints in your proposal in this section. And for each risk and constraint, describe the mitigation plan so the readers know you have thought through how to clear the obstacles to be successful with your business case.

Finally, list the assumptions you have about the proposal. This may be a preliminary list at this point and grow with more detailed planning, but at least demonstrate that you have given some thought to the assumptions.

Alternatives Analysis

In addition to presenting a recommendation, you should always include a summary of the alternatives you considered. Be brief but objective. Explain why the alternatives were rejected in favor of your recommendation.

Implementation Plan

The implementation plan describes how you will accomplish the recommended course of action. It should at least include the major milestones and the targeted completion dates. Indicate that a detailed project plan with more precise completion dates is forthcoming.

Approvals

Finally, add a section where you can demonstrate your approvals. Simply list the names and titles of the people responsible for approving your business case.

Generally speaking, the more expensive your proposal, the more you may need to meet with stakeholders beforehand and provide a verbal summary of what you are proposing. It's important to know your audience and understand people's individual preferences.

A sample business-case template is available on the companion website.

Package Innovation

Over the course of my career, I discovered a paradox between users who demand more frequent changes to enterprise software (e.g., enterprise resource planning or customer relationship management) and users—sometimes the same ones—who complain that IT changes the systems too often. I'm sure you've heard a user complain, "Just when I got comfortable using the system, IT changed it!"

The answer may be to package changes into less frequent internal releases of your systems. For instance, consider moving to *quarterly* releases instead of daily, weekly, or even monthly releases. While this release management methodology may seem shocking at first, it's actually quite efficient and has many benefits.

Windsor CIO Boyd used IT infrastructure library and COBIT processes to help his company transition from daily to monthly software releases. "Moving to monthly releases has forced the business to improve its planning and resulted in better quality software products at a lower price point," says Gary. He is now working with his team to evaluate a move to quarterly releases. "Moving from daily to monthly was a massive challenge in terms of business adoption. Now that people are accustomed to less frequent change and we demonstrated the value, it should not be as difficult to move to a quarterly process," he adds.

The quarterly release methodology becomes even more compelling if you have many integration points between applications. The more integration you have, the more changes and testing you are likely to encounter. Testing is expensive; it takes resources away from other tasks, sometimes for several days or weeks. Even though automated test scripts can relieve some of the burden, you still face all of the other administrative duties involved in managing a release, including deploying the code to the various environments, preparing release notes, updating documentation, creating training materials, and training the support team.

IT leaders need to acknowledge the fact that releases are not only about the software. Other administrative aspects involved in a release can make it very expensive if not properly planned. Software releases are not that different from packaging a consumer product; many of the same administrative steps are applicable. The DVD player you see on the shelf at Best Buy didn't get there because someone in the research and development group at Sony had an epiphany yesterday and then poof, it was on the shelf! A lot of design, development, testing, and packaging went into the effort.

IT leaders need to acknowledge the fact that releases are not only about the software. Other administrative aspects involved in a release can make it very expensive if not properly planned.

The Upside of Quarterly Releases

The following is a list of benefits of moving to quarterly software releases:

- Improves end-user awareness and adoption of changes.
- Ensures changes are aligned with long-term business objectives.
- Allows for better resource planning and allocation.
- Reduces the risk of introducing defects into the production environment.
- Reduces change-control administration costs.
- Ensures compliance to company internal standards and policies and external laws.
- Provides an opportunity to create a theme for releases, such as ease of use functionality, performance improvements, or functionality to support a major project.
- Improves the coordination of integrated functionality to streamline and automate work flow.

The Downside of Quarterly Releases

Of course, there are also disadvantages to the quarterly software releases, including upsetting the users who want the changes as soon as they are ready for production. In their opinion, delaying a change is unacceptable, since they want or even need it to be available for use immediately.

Complexity Drives Frequency

Conair CIO Harding says that "the complexity of the platform is a key driver in determining the frequency at which changes should be considered." He explains that he is running a single global instance of SAP at Conair across North America, South America, Europe, and the Far East without many bolt-on systems. He adds, "The simplicity of our software portfolio allows us to make more frequent changes without the worry that an integration point may break due to a change. That being said, we are planning more integration with software-as-a-service providers, which may lead us to reevaluate the frequency of our software releases."

Fast-Tracking Changes

A way of managing the "need it now" mentality for enhancements is to create a process to fast-track certain types of changes to production. A good example of a fast track is a change that enables a business to meet a new regulatory requirement.

There are some applications, particularly in the arena of customer relationship management, that cannot wait days or weeks, let alone months, for changes. For instance, online retailers may not want to delay changes to their website more than a day or a week. Not all applications are created equal, so you will need to evaluate your portfolio to identify the appropriate deployment practice for each application.

Reports are another category where there is questionable value in a long delay in making a change to the production system. Typically, there is less administrative work in deploying a report change to production. In fact, in some instances, users can promote reports on their own. Some IT shops have considered more frequent releases of reports but have at least moved away from daily releases for the benefits stated previously. A good compromise is to move to weekly or monthly releases for report *changes* only, although I recommend that *new* reports be folded into quarterly releases.

Take-Two Interactive CIO Hinkle has settled on a weekly release cycle for internal software, but most of the changes that go into his releases are related to reports. "If I have six changes going into our production environment this weekend, five will be changes to reports," he says.

The Implications of Using Software-as-a-Service Providers

Less frequent software releases can also be vexing if many of your systems are integrating with software-as-a-service (SAAS) providers—that is, off-premise application providers. Your success with your release management strategy will depend on your contractual and working relationships with your providers so that you can coordinate changes based on your schedule, not theirs. For instance, you wouldn't want a provider changing its software before you are ready to test it as part of your release schedule. With careful planning and partnering, you can successfully implement an integrated release strategy with a SAAS deployment model.

As an IT leader, you will need to be discerning and examine the costs and benefits of your release management strategy and choose what is appropriate for your company. It is somewhat of a cultural issue; some users may just be accustomed to getting access to the changes as soon as they are ready, despite the inefficiencies. These cultural issues can be buffeted by examining and communicating the costs and benefits of various strategies and selecting the strategy that works best for your organization.

Go Green

Over the last decade or so, organizations of various shapes and sizes have been cutting waste, reducing costs, and improving their effect on the environment. There are many methods of using technology to become a greener company, such as virtualization, video conferencing, paperless processes, PC and printer power management, and data center equipment efficiencies. Despite the many types of green products and services, however, green IT still requires a lot of heavy lifting from your IT department.

According to Gartner Group, emerging markets are growing rapidly in terms of technology expenditures and influence. Growing technology use and energy consumption around the globe have led to an increased emphasis on green technologies and power conservation within IT industries.[9]

Richard Lattmann is the associate vice president of infrastructure services for the U.S. affiliate of Sanofi, a diversified global health-care leader with nearly 100,000 dedicated professionals in more than 100 countries. I met with Rich to ask about his efforts with greening IT at Sanofi. This is what he told me:

First, I should mention that we recently transformed from having a decentralized infrastructure, organized around businesses and geographies, to a global infrastructure organization. Greening IT has been a core directive for our new organization, and we have made significant progress in this area by virtualizing our server farm, which reduced our power consumption and carbon footprint. We are also planning to consolidate our twenty-six data centers down to three, which will lead to further savings. As significant as these efforts have been for IT, they don't get much attention from the business because they are out of sight.

Interestingly, the smaller things that we have done with greening IT have actually created more awareness. As an example, we were finding stacks of print output sitting by our printers and never getting picked up. It was surprising to us that so many people weren't picking up what they were printing. It was such a waste of paper, ink, and power. We are now piloting a program to have our printers only print output when the employee approaches the printer and waves their card key ID badge. The added benefit with this approach is that it supports mobility and confidentiality because an employee can send a print command from their mobile device when they are on the road and then print the output when they arrive at the office.

Green IT is here to stay, even in a difficult economic environment. Energy will be one of the preeminent public concerns of the next decade, and energy conservation will be an integral part of the solution. Going green is not only about being environmentally responsible; it is also a strategy that has tangible business and economic benefits. To achieve the benefits of greening IT in your organization, start by making it a strategic goal and then set clear and concise personal objectives that are cascaded throughout your team. Keeping green front and center will help you exploit opportunities to contribute to this effort.

Top Plays

- To capitalize on innovation in a competitive global economy, CIOs must solve today's problems yesterday by seizing opportunities to leverage emerging technologies.
- Effective governance leverages the ingenuity of people.

(continued)

- Summits bring together people from multiple committees to work through cross-functional issues.
- IT is expected to demonstrate the possibilities that technology can offer to an organization.
- Being innovative doesn't always mean being the first to come up with the idea. It is a new interpretation of something.
- Think big and create a culture of innovation throughout your company.
- Business cases serve as input into governance committees.
- Software releases are not just about software. Other aspects involved in a release can make them very expensive if not properly planned.

Notes

1. Arthur VanGundy, *Getting to Innovation: How Asking the Right Questions Generates the Great Ideas Your Company Needs* (New York: Amacom, 2007), xi–xii.
2. Peter Weill and Jeanne W. Ross, *IT Governance: How Top Performers Manage IT Decision Rights for Superior Results* (Boston: Harvard Business School Publishing, 2004), 2.
3. Walter Isaacson, *Steve Jobs* (New York: Simon & Schuster, 2011), 138.
4. Julia King, "When IT Gets to Play: Skunk Works Projects Deliver Value," *ComputerWorld*, December 5, 2011.
5. Julia King, "Chief of the Year," *CIO*, December 12, 2011.
6. Peter Skarzynski and Rowan Gibson, *Innovation to the Core: A Blueprint For Transforming the Way Your Company Innovates* (Boston: Harvard Business Press, 2008), 3–4.
7. Robert Cringely, *Triumph of the Nerds: How the Personal Computer Changed the World* (DVD), PBS, 1996.
8. Gary, Hamel, *Leading the Revolution: How to Thrive in Turbulent Times by Making Innovation a Way of Life* (Boston: Harvard Business School Press, 2000), 16–17.
9. Daryl C. Plummer and Peter Middleton, "Predicts 2012: Four Forces Combine to Transform the IT Landscape," Gartner Group, December 9, 2011, http://www.gartner.com/id=1871420.

Chapter 4

Step 4: Deliver

Vision without action is a daydream. Action without vision is a nightmare.
—Japanese proverb

Deliver: Implement products and services to improve bottom-line performance for your company.

Chapter 3 discussed how IT can partner with the rest of the business to develop innovative solutions. Acquiring and developing technology is one thing, however; successfully delivering it to employees across an organization is an entirely different matter. Perhaps we should spend less time talking about strategic planning, priority setting, and developing technology and more time talking about operational excellence and how to achieve it. T. S. Eliot once said, "In the annals of innovation, new ideas are only part of the equation. Execution is just as important."

This chapter discusses the operational practices necessary for successfully delivering results. One of the most significant challenges for CIOs is successfully implementing global enterprise systems, such as enterprise resource planning (ERP), customer relationship management (CRM), and supply chain management (SCM). For that reason, I decided to focus this chapter on this topic.

Also, while you and your team may always deliver high-quality products and services, you may not always get the recognition that you deserve. For that reason, this chapter discusses how to create an IT marketing program to set expectations with your business partners and communicate progress with goals and objectives.

Why System Implementations Fail

In general, the simplest definition of failure consists of projects that are late, are over budget, or do not deliver planned benefits. According to a study conducted in 2011, 61 percent of ERP projects take longer than expected. An average of 74 percent of the projects exceed budget, and less than 50 percent of them do not realize their intended benefits.[1]

ERP projects continue to face implementation challenges and difficulties; misplaced expectations of time and budget drive dramatic overruns on many projects. At the same time, more companies experienced benefits from the ERP implementations, suggesting increased priority on this critical point, which is ultimately the most important of all.[2] As more companies look to invest in deploying enterprise systems, CIOs need to build awareness of the best practices to ensure success.

There are many reasons for enterprise system failures. Here is a list of 10 typical reasons (in no particular order):

1. Lack of project sponsorship
2. Poorly defined scope
3. Inexperienced project manager or team
4. Insufficient staff
5. Poor teamwork
6. Lack of a business case
7. Poor project plan and methodology
8. Unrealistic effort estimation

9. Insufficient funding
10. Poor communication

Develop a High-Performance Team

One of the most significant pitfalls of enterprise system projects is a lack of effective teamwork (item number 5 in the above list). In his acclaimed book *The Five Dysfunctions of a Team: A Leadership Fable*, Patrick Lencioni described five distinct reasons why teams fail. The five dysfunctions of a team form a pyramid; from the bottom up, they are (1) absence of trust, (2) fear of conflict, (3) lack of commitment, (4) avoidance of account-ability, and (5) inattention to results. Lencioni wrote the following on how to build a successful team:

> And so, like a chain with just one link broken, teamwork deteriorates if even a single dysfunction is allowed to flourish.
>
> Another way to understand this model is to take the opposite approach—a positive one—and imagine how members of truly cohesive teams behave:
>
> - They trust one another.
> - They engage in unfiltered conflict around ideas.
> - They commit to decisions and plans of action.
> - They hold one another accountable for delivering against those plans.
> - They focus on the achievement of collective results.
>
> If this sounds simple, it's because it is simple, at least in theory. In practice, however, it is extremely difficult because it requires levels of discipline and persistence that few teams can muster.[3]

One of the most significant pitfalls of enterprise system projects is a lack of effective teamwork.

I talked with Michael Del Priore, the vice president and Global CIO of Church & Dwight Company, and I learned that one of the initiatives he identified as part of his strategic planning process was the launch of a global ERP system and data warehouse. I asked Michael about the strategies that helped the company be successful with the initiative. Here is what he said:

> *First, we made sure there was organizational commitment to the program from the most senior levels in the company—right down to the individuals involved in the project on a full-time basis. Second, we avoided the issue of the program being viewed as a technology initiative by assigning the VP of manufacturing as the program leader. Finally, we established master data management and business integration teams tasked with ensuring high-quality data and providing training and support services to end users postimplementation.*

Develop a Team-Building Program

Working on a newly formed team is a lot like experiencing the first day in a new school. You don't learn much the first day because you are too busy with finding your locker and your classrooms and making new friends. The early days of a new team can be equally unproductive as members struggle with learning the goals and objectives and their responsibilities.

In many system implementations, people from various departments are asked to work with people in other departments for the very first time over a course of months—or even years. While some of the members may know others, it is not unusual to find that most people have not worked together very closely or for an extended period. In these cases, I generally like to conduct a team-building event to get the team to gel and to make sure everyone is aligned on a common set of goals and objectives. An effective program can be a great way to help your team get off on the right track.

> Individual commitment to a group effort—that is what makes a team work, a company work, a society work, a civilization work.
> —Vince Lombardi

Most teambuilding programs are a blend of in-classroom learning and adventure experiences. The key is to offer a lot of interactivity and to make it an enjoyable learning experience as well as an opportunity for the participants to get to know one another on a personal level. People learn differently, so by offering a curriculum that includes a variety of learning methods, you will improve your chances of success.

For most of my large-scale enterprise system implementations, I have worked with outside consultants to develop and conduct a custom team-building program that takes place over two or three days. A typical program consists of the following topics:

- The executive sponsor gives a talk on the importance of the project and how it will help the company meet its goals. In the best cases, the CEO attends to kick off the program.
- The CIO gives a similar talk to demonstrate his or her support of the project.
- The program facilitator reviews the agenda with the attendees.
- The project manager reviews the milestones of the project. I am assuming that the team-building program is conducted after the project plan has been developed and the team is staffed.
- The facilitator conducts an exercise to help the team members understand and appreciate different learning styles. To save time, you can have the participants complete a personality test ahead of time, such as the Myers-Briggs Type Indicator assessment.
- Experiential exercises foster the importance of working as a team. When I worked at Pepsi-Cola in the 1990s, we had the slogan "The Power of One," which signified that you are more powerful as a team if you work together toward a common vision. You can demonstrate the power of teamwork through physical exercises such as a relay race or more cerebral exercises such as a puzzle.
- Every team will inevitably face problems that the members will need to solve together. The question is whether the members will communicate effectively with one another when confronted with new challenges. Experiential exercises can be conducted to help the team with problem solving and communication.

Throughout the years, I have found that some team members are reluctant to participate in such a program because they believe it's a waste of time or money. Invariably, these are the same people who come out of the program with the greatest learning experience and appreciation for the program. I have experienced people tearing up at the end of the program because they learned so much about themselves and their new teammates.

Organizational development firms are an invaluable source of expertise on team building and management development, since they spend their days coaching organizations on how to develop high-performance teams and individuals. Over the course of my career, I have been privileged to work with some of the best people in the business. I am truly grateful that they spent time with me sharing their insights on a variety of topics. Their good advice and counsel are interspersed throughout this book.

Jeff Boyd is the president of Operation Explore, an experiential training and organizational development company that serves a diversified client base, including many Fortune 100 companies. I asked Jeff about the best practices in developing an effective team-building program. This is what he shared with me:

> *The need for forming highly collaborative teams is more important than ever due to the shift to a global economy. A critical aspect in team development that has been undervalued is building the communities or relationships that lead to increased trust and an appreciation of cultural differences. I am working on a team-building program for a large pharmaceutical company, involving participants from Japan, Europe, and multiple states in the U.S.*
>
> *As part of the research for the program, we have learned that the Japanese participants prefer not to write things down because of the strict regulatory concerns in the pharmaceutical industry. As you can imagine, this can lead to communication issues and frustration for the rest of the team. So we are helping the team develop an awareness and understanding of this cultural difference and then developing techniques for the team to use for communicating with each other.*
>
> *Another challenge that we find with teams is the habit of talking with a third party when there is a challenge with a teammate. We encourage team members to be direct with each other and to be very clear when defining and verbally communicating goals, objectives, and progress with the project. Sometimes you need to pull things to the forefront for everyone to recognize and accept.*
>
> *The metaphor we share is: "Imagine that you are watching a football game with some friends and you are really enjoying the game, then someone points out some static, such as a line across the TV screen. Others may not have noticed the line, but now that it was illuminated it becomes hard to not*

notice it. Now instead of watching and enjoying the game they are watching and getting distracted by the line on the screen."

By being direct with a teammate versus talking about a teammate with another person, you avoid pointing out deficiencies for someone else to notice.

Kevin Nash is the president of Aspen Organization Development Consulting, a boutique consulting firm specializing in helping organizations, teams, and individuals reach peak performance. Bringing its clients a wealth of practical knowledge and experience, Aspen specializes in talent management, change management, and employee training and development consulting services. I asked Kevin for his suggestions on building an effective team-building program. Kevin has what he likes to call an evidenced-based approach to developing his programs:

> *We created a Team 360 program that is designed to probe the effectiveness of the team based on feedback from various stakeholders, including sponsors, steering committee members, vendors, and team members. The survey is conducted at multiple points throughout a project to identify the critical successful factors as well as to form a baseline of performance. We ask questions such as "How well are the objectives of the project understood?" and "Is the team working effectively?"*
>
> *Identifying issues early in the project life cycle allows you to take corrective action to remediate the issues. The results are captured in a database so that the organization can report on the factors that contribute to success or failure of their projects. We also conduct follow-up interviews with the stakeholders to try to uncover other factors that contributed to the outcome of the project. All of the information goes into a knowledge base that is available to the client so it can be leveraged to help guide future projects.*

Jeff has some tips about things to avoid when you're developing a team-building program:

> *As a facilitator of a team-building program, you should never go into a session unprepared. A simple example is to assume that the members don't already know each other and then waste time with introductions.*
>
> *Another example is to make goals as overt as possible, so that everyone can buy into them. I have had clients who were notorious for having "covert" goals. The client comes to us with the desire to work on the leadership teams' level of challenge with their people, but he did not want us to come out and*

say that. This put me in a difficult position of trying to satisfy both parties by getting the desired behaviors without openly discussing the objectives for the program.

Also, don't try to jam a program into one day when you know it requires at least two days or even a process that continues on. The example that I share is: "It is like joining a gym and you work out once and expect to have a washboard stomach." You will more than likely fall short of achieving the goals of the program and disappoint the participants and the project sponsors.

Finally, I discourage conducting a team-building event as a form of intervention for one team member who is a challenge. These situations are best handled using individual coaching. In the end, the more overt you can be about a team-building program, the more successful you will be with the outcome.

Kevin thinks that communicating the value proposition of a team-building program and getting people to understand what's in it for them is the key to its success:

Adults really need to see the value of what they are learning and how to apply it for results. If you are being too theoretical, you will lose the participants right from the beginning. You want to avoid having people feel they are being put through a car wash—meaning, they may come out of a team-building event feeling a little cleaner, but they really haven't learned anything that they can immediately apply. A good approach is to get some of the influencers within the group to participate in the design of the program or even the presentation of the material. This helps you establish realistic goals and the necessary buy-in for the program.

I am sure you have been involved in a few team-building events over the course of your career. Have you found that even though the programs appeared to help people open up and build trust, the effects of the program tended to wear off soon after the people returned to their jobs? I asked Jeff and Kevin about some of the techniques that they use to make the lessons learned from a program last. Jeff says the following:

Your success with the long-term benefits of the program begins with the upfront due diligence in defining the objectives and desired outcomes. I begin my work with a data collection process that involves interviewing the key stakeholders, which helps me to understand the challenges that they are facing and their expectations for the program. It also helps to build rapport and gives the stakeholders some accountability for the success of the program.

Your success depends on whether you have established effective mechanisms to monitor progress after the program.

For example, at the end of the program, I ask each participant to identify a behavior that he or she wants to improve based upon what they learned about themselves. They share the goal with their supervisor and monitor progress through normal performance management review processes.

Another process is to have the facilitator of the program "check in" with the program members within one to three months after the program to understand if progress is being made. I encourage teams to create "rules of engagement," which is essentially a list of behavioral statements that the team agrees will set them up for success. This is a living, breathing document that is used as a guide for team effectiveness. The most successful teams use the rules of engagement as a metric for team performance and evaluate the team on the statements. Going through the development of the rules of engagement and building sweat equity are just as important as the statements themselves.

There is not one method that will help you sustain the benefits of the program. The trick is to apply multiple pressure points to keep the lessons learned in the forefront of everyone's mind.

Kevin believes that organizational culture can make or break your ability to realize the benefits of a team-building program:

The success of a team-building program ultimately depends upon whether the organizational culture is supportive of the learned behaviors. If you spent the last few days encouraging a team to become more trusting of others, but the culture back at the office is politically charged, where most people have a Machiavellian approach to conflict, then people will likely revert back to their old behaviors.

On the other hand, if the culture is supportive of teamwork, you should link whatever was learned in the program to the individual's performance management plan so that you measure progress. Weaving the new desired behaviors into the company's performance review or personal development planning program makes it a natural extension of an existing process and not something entirely new and burdensome to absorb and monitor.

In summary, while there are many reasons enterprise system implementations fail, there is only one reason they succeed: people. If a team leader is able to build a team of people who are trusting of one another and are selflessly and genuinely focused on the same goals and objectives, he or she has a very good chance of succeeding.

Discover Organizational Readiness

Once you have collaborated with the governance committees to design and develop an enterprise system and have staffed your implementation team, you are ready to start rolling out the system across the organization.

Enterprise systems are typically used for the purpose of transitioning an organization to a common set of business processes and systems so as to realize the benefits of a common operating platform. This section discusses the best practices involved in implementing enterprise systems across the company. For the purposes of instruction, it assumes that the organization is made up of divisions operating in the same line of business but currently using different systems and processes. The same, or very similar, practices can be applied to other scenarios, such as divisions operating in different lines of business. Some of the steps would require more due diligence, however, such as additional discovery of processes.

This section also assumes that the selection and configuration of the standard enterprise system has already been completed using the innovation practices mentioned in Chapter 3. That being said, the system may need additional configuration to support local regulatory and business requirements. So when I mention steps such as *design* and *develop*, I am referring to applying mission critical changes but not sacrificing standard processes or software configuration to conform to the way the business unit currently operates.

The discover phase is an initial step in any enterprise system implementation. It helps the team capture and understand a division's current business processes, systems, data integrity, infrastructure, cultural preparedness, skill sets, and resource availability for the purposes of defining the scope, plan, costs, and benefits of an implementation.

Even though the governance committees defined the new solution, the team must assume that each division is operating differently (hence the need for a standard system) and thus make an effort to discover the differences for the purposes of converting data and managing the transition. Unfortunately, many projects fail because insufficient efforts are devoted to identifying, analyzing, documenting, and validating the "as is" practices in a division.

The discover phase includes three major activities: feasibility, process and operational findings, and scope and approach. Of course, the amount of project management time required is proportional to the size of the project; typically, the effort takes one to three months, depending on the size and complexity of the organization as well as the availability of resources.

Feasibility

The objective of the feasibility activity is to identify the readiness of the organization to begin an enterprise system implementation. To do this, the team performs the following tasks:

- **Introduction to management.** A high-level presentation of the new business processes and systems is provided to key management stakeholders so they can begin to understand how work will be performed in the new environment. This is not a demonstration of the software but rather an overview of the new standard business processes and their inherent interrelationships.
- **Overview of implementation methodology.** It is important that employees understand the step-by-step plan for phasing in the new operating platform. While the full project plan has not been developed at this early stage, the team can at least present the detailed plan for the discover phase and briefly outline the steps that are undertaken in the develop-and-implement phase (e.g., develop or convert). In addition, the change management program is discussed and emphasized in this phase.
- **Organizational structure review.** In this task, the team examines the organizational chart and existing job descriptions to determine the management hierarchy and job roles that exist in the division. This is an important task, because it helps the team to do the following:
  - Identify the stakeholders who need to be targeted for surveys and interviews.
  - Compare the existing job roles to the enterprise system job roles to understand the training implications.

- Begin to understand the requirements for a security model.
- Understand the governance structure to determine future membership on teams such as the project steering committee and site project team.

    It is critical that the project team identify the "opinion leaders" in a division. Opinion leaders are the most influential members of any group or organization, and they aren't always in management positions. Other people tend to follow the behaviors of opinion leaders. In order to lead a group—especially a large group—you will benefit from identifying the opinion leaders and recruiting their help.

- **Questionnaire of existing processes and operations.** In this task, a questionnaire is designed and distributed to the department heads in the division to begin to understand how the work is currently performed and how operational decisions are made throughout the division. This information is assembled further through interviews in the subsequent process and operational findings activity.
- **Resource availability for the project.** A determination is made of the level of skilled resources that need to be assigned to the project and whether those resources exist. At this time, the team is not expected to have a concise resource plan, so the objective here is to get a sense of resource capacity to support the initiative.
- **Business operations and plans.** Discussions take place to understand the current operations and the business plan for the next several years. Is the division planning on any major changes in the coming months while your team is in the middle of a conversion?
- **Data evaluation.** Take time to gain an understanding of data sources, data owners, and systems in the division. Develop a system map and a data dictionary; describing the systems and key data elements that are available in the legacy systems is a particularly helpful exercise in identifying data redundancy and the system of record for data elements.
- **User skills assessment.** An early step in any project is to understand the business process and technical skills of the targeted users and to prepare for the eventual training program. Individual skills, such as basic PC skills, are also identified in order to determine specific prerequisite training needs.

- **Determination of satisfaction with existing business processes and systems.** Surveys are conducted to gain an understanding of the division's satisfaction with existing business processes and systems so that an early benchmark can be developed. Users tend to have fond memories of their legacy systems once they begin using a new system and are struggling with the learning curve. It's handy to be able to reference the survey results to remind users of where they came from, particularly if they reported low satisfaction with their legacy system.

- **Site visits to previously implemented divisions.** Stakeholders participate in on-site visits to divisions already working with the new processes and systems so that they can get a picture of the outcome and gain some insight from their peers who have already been through the implementation process. If site visits aren't possible, then at least encourage the users to call their peers in another division that's running the system.

- **Infrastructure assessment.** The division's infrastructure is evaluated and a document is written to describe the physical entities, such as office buildings, communities, training facilities, telecommunications capabilities, and computer systems. This task should be performed early in the discover phase because of the lead time required to address any gaps in telecommunications and to understand the logistics of the various locations so the implementation team can better prepare for travel arrangements.

- **Review of compliance audits.** In this activity, the team examines previous audit reports to determine the division's adherence to operational policies and procedures. The team should also make time to meet with the auditing department to gather further intelligence about the current compliance of the targeted division. The meetings are helpful in gaining insight into how the division collaborates with other corporate functions and the general culture of the company. Are the employees in the division responsive? Do they follow up on assigned tasks? Do they react positively or negatively to corporate engagement? Also as part of this task, the team collects local policies and procedures, if available, to determine whether there are any differences from companywide policies and procedures.

- **Review of findings.** The final step in the discover phase is a meeting with the division's management and corporate management to present the findings. A decision is made on whether the project should continue based on the findings or if further action is needed before proceeding.

Opinion leaders are the most influential members of any group or organization, and they aren't always in management positions.

Process and Operational Findings

The objective of the process and operational findings activity is to gain an understanding for the current ("as is") processes that exist in the division, the operational meetings used to make decisions, and the reports that are used to support those decisions. The purpose of the activity is to compare and contrast the current environment to the new environment and determine if any gaps exist (e.g., statutory requirements) that need to be considered as part of the scope of the project.

Again, the purpose of an enterprise system implementation is to transition the organization to align with company policies, standard business processes, and systems to realize the benefits of a common operating platform. It is not the intention to re-create reports or the functionality existing in legacy systems because people are comfortable with the old way of doing things. This is a business transformation project, not an IT project, and will require a great deal of transition management. There are seven steps involved in kicking off a project in a business unit:

1. **Introduction to the full staff.** A high-level presentation of the enterprise system business processes and systems is performed for all employees in the division as part of a staff meeting. This activity helps the broader audience gain an understanding of how work is performed in the new environment. This is not a detailed demonstration of the software; rather, it is an overview of the new business processes and their inherent interrelationships. A low-cost and effective method of achieving this objective is through the use of an e-learning module.

2. **In-person interviews.** While the responses to the questionnaires in the earlier activity help to establish the foundation of information on existing processes and operations, they do not allow for interaction and follow-up questions. For this, the team conducts in-person interviews with division staff to learn more about how the work is performed and how operational decisions are made.

   Upon completion of the in-person interviews, a brief summary is presented to the interviewees to confirm an understanding of the information acquired.

3. **Observation.** Interviews give the employees an opportunity to tell you how the work is performed in their divisions, but physical observations show you how the work is performed. I often discover that work is executed differently from what a manager may believe is happening, so this exercise can be enlightening for both you and the division you are implementing your system in. For this reason, make a practice of traveling to various sites within a division to observe the work being performed by the employees. Also, attend operational meetings to get a firsthand impression of the current forums for sharing information and making decisions. While this time is mainly used to observe operations, use the opportunity to ask questions based on your observations, survey results, and interview responses to validate the information.

4. **Collection of material.** Even though surveys and interviews are an excellent way of gathering information, be sure to collect actual samples of materials such as existing reports, process maps, training material, system documentation, and paper forms.

5. **Gap analysis.** Gap analysis is the study of the difference between two different information systems or applications, often for the purpose of determining how to get from one state to a new state. A gap is sometimes spoken of as "the space between where we are and where we want to be." Gap analysis is undertaken as a means of bridging that space.

   Based on the results of the questionnaires, interviews, and observations, a gap analysis is conducted by comparing the current division practices with the new business processes and systems to determine if any issues need to be addressed in order to achieve a successful implementation. For instance, a division may have statutory requirements that need to be adhered to in the system that may not have already been designed.

6. **Process and report mapping.** As part of the design of your training program, consider building lessons that offer comparisons of "as is" with "to be" to help the employees transition to the new environment. Be sure to cross-reference significant "as is" processes, terms, and reports to the related "to be" entities in the new environment.

7. **Presentation of findings.** One of the most important tasks for the project team is to explain the purpose of the outcome it is seeking. It is not uncommon for people to have difficulty understanding the purpose of the project because they do not have a realistic idea of where the organization really stands compared to divisions that have implemented the solution. At this stage, present observations and recommendations to the division's management and corporate management. A decision is made on whether the project should continue based on the findings or if further action is needed before proceeding.

The purpose of an enterprise system implementation is to transition the organization to align with company policies, standard business processes, and systems to realize the benefits of a common operating platform.

Scope and Approach

The final deliverables of the discover phase is the project definition and work plan for the subsequent develop-and-implement phase of the enterprise system rollout. It is important to gain consensus on the scope and approach of the project before initiating the develop-and-implement phase, and a formal sign-off should be achieved with leadership representatives from both the division and corporate management. The discover phase results in the creation of the following documents:

- **Required process and systems changes.** In the process and operational findings activity, you identified gaps (e.g., statutory requirements) in the new system that must be resolved before the system can be implemented in the division. In this task, the team documents these changes so they can be designed and developed into the new system as part of the implementation phase.

- **Business-benefits statement.** The objective in this task is to describe the value the division can realize from the implementation. The statement is developed in cooperation with the division leaders. The statement includes a schedule of required project resources (internal and external). In many cases, most of the benefits have already been established and documented by the governance committees. So the implementation team may just need to add a few more points based on findings during the discover phase.
- **Risk management plan.** A reactive project manager tries to resolve issues when they occur. A proactive project manager tries to resolve problems before they occur. Developing a risk management plan involves proactively identifying risks, building a contingency plan, and monitoring the execution of risk activities.
- **Communication plan.** For many small and medium projects, status reports and status meetings may be all that is required for formal communication. However, on a large project, you need to incorporate communications within the context of an overall communications plan. The rationale behind a well-thought-out communication plan is that it is much easier to implement a solution when people are informed and excited about a new system rather than when they are confused, frightened, or ambivalent. A communication plan is used to build enthusiasm and usually includes newsletters, presentations, team-building events, and the celebration of major milestones.
- **Data conversion plan.** Data conversions typically include leveraging business data—usually found in many disparate systems—and transforming it so that it can be loaded into the enterprise system. This document describes the sources of data and the transformation plan (e.g., data mapping).
- **Project organization.** This document describes the project team and governing bodies that will guide and support the project, including named resources from corporate management and from the division to participate in the project.

- **Security plan.** At this stage, the team should provide a document describing the list of job roles for the targeted division and the key security-related activities and milestones.
- **Budget schedule.** The project management team is responsible for developing, managing, and tracking project-related costs. In this activity, you should build a budget for the implementation phase, including the costs of licenses, maintenance, travel, training, and consulting. Specify which costs are the responsibility of the division and which are the responsibility of the implementation team.

Develop and Implement

The develop-and-implement phase of an enterprise system rollout typically consists of the following major activities: design, development, conversion, testing, and support.

It includes the execution of the plans discussed in the scope and approach activity (e.g., the communication, conversion, and security plans). Since this isn't a book on software development practices, I will just briefly touch on the major activities involved in the develop-and-implement phase:

- **Design.** As a result of the discovery phase, you identified changes required for the new system to address gaps. Some of the changes may just be process changes that need to be incorporated into the training material. Use this activity to design each of the changes (process and/or system).
- **Development.** Once your team has designed all of the required process and system changes, the specifications are handed over to the development function in your department. Any changes should also be properly documented and included in the training materials.
- **Conversion.** The data conversion step is often underestimated, so be sure that plenty of time is allocated for this step. Conversions require sufficient planning and resources to extract, translate, and load data into the new system. Also, make certain there is ample time for users to validate the data once it has been converted. Too

often, this critical step is compressed at the end of the develop-and-implement phase, and users end up validating data after the system is live. This creates an enormous risk because the business begins to transact with the incorrect data. With the proper planning and resource capacity, a team can tackle data conversion and avoid heroics later.

- **Testing.** Any new features incorporated into the software obviously need to be properly tested. Since we are focusing on the topic of *enterprise* systems, the team needs to be certain that the changes to accommodate the new division don't have an adverse effect on the other divisions running the system. It's always a good practice to include users from the other divisions in the user–acceptance testing activity.

| The journey only begins with the launch of a new enterprise system.

- **Training.** Not unlike the philosophy to *run IT like a business*, a best practice is for companies to transform training from *running as a function* to *running like a business*. That is the key to delivering training, the kind of value that results-minded executives recognize, appreciate, respect, and increasingly demand.[4] Those who have worked with me know that I have a tremendous passion for training. Whether systems training is delivered by IT or by another business function, the courses should be defined and described in a role-based curriculum (e.g., controller, sales consultant, or purchasing manager) so that all the employees know exactly what is being offered to them to acquire the knowledge and skills for their roles.

  As new employees join the company or move to other roles, you should require them to complete a set of courses before being given access to system functionality for the first time. Some companies are quite sophisticated in this area and require their employees to complete online courses and pass tests, or they rely on the staff to provide the instructor-led training. Whatever your delivery mechanism may be, you will most likely see a reduction in help desk tickets and a higher level of user productivity if you require training before system access. User communities should take responsibility for training employees on business software applications and related processes. The practice of establishing a super user program for this purpose is discussed in Chapter 5.

A similar training strategy should be established to support the educational needs of your IT staff. This subject is described further in Chapter 7.

- **Support.** Chapter 5 is dedicated to the goal of providing superior support services to your business partners, suppliers, and customers. The journey only begins with the launch of a new enterprise system. So it's imperative that you provide on-site support for several weeks to be sure the users are acclimating to the new processes and software functionality. You have turned their world upside down, so even the most basic tasks, such as creating a purchase order, require more time and energy as they combat the learning curve.

The data conversion step is often underestimated, so be sure that plenty of time is allocated for this step.

Get Insanely Motivated

If you have ever implemented an enterprise system, you know it is extremely difficult. You need a great plan, strong sponsors, cultural awareness, a big budget, and, most important of all, an insanely motivated team. You need "doers," people who are relentlessly focused on the goal of delivering the system on time and within budget. This is not to say that you should count on heroics throughout the entire project cycle, but there are moments when heroics are required.

Doers exude passion, confidence, drive, a strong work ethic, and loyalty. They inspire others to work hard and take the risks needed to deliver results.

What you want to avoid at all costs are the "naysayers." These people are generally characterized as pessimistic, unhappy, and negative, and they are poison to the rest of your team. You need to identify the naysayers and pluck them out of your organization as soon as you can or risk having them spread their cynicism and negativity to the rest of your team and reducing the much-needed productivity.

Just Say No

No is the most important word you need to learn when rolling out enterprise systems. Why is it so important to say no? The moment you define the scope and approach of your project, someone—maybe even your boss—will inevitably try to add something to your plate. I call these "distractions" or "noise." Enterprise system rollouts take enormous focus. The moment you start expanding the scope of the implementation or take on other "special projects" is the moment you start to go off course.

I once joined a company that was attempting to implement a system across the United States. It had assembled a project team that was supposedly dedicated to the project on a full-time basis. Within a week of being on the job, I identified over twenty "special projects" they were working on that had absolutely nothing to do with the enterprise system rollout. It was costing the organization valuable time and money because it meant that internal resources and consulting resources would be assigned to the project for a longer period. It also meant that the benefits of the new system would be delayed. Why did this happen in the first place? The previous project director didn't know how to say no.

Of course, if your boss asks you to take on additional responsibilities or adds more to the scope of your project, it's not always so easy to say no. But you have to at least try to explain the risks that the additional work would create for the project.

In *The 11 Secrets of Highly Influential IT Leaders*, Marc J. Schiller told a story about when he met Walter Peltz, the former CIO of Medco, and it provides an interesting perspective on how one CIO learned how to focus on what is important to the business and not get distracted with a lot of noise:

> I was escorted to his [Walter's] office and the very first thing I noticed was how empty it was. Almost no books on the shelves, no pictures, no decorative ornaments. The desk was completely clean. It looked and felt like an unoccupied office.
>
> After the usual introductions, I casually asked, "Is this a new office for you? Did your group recently move?" Walter responded by saying, "Given how often I have to say 'no' to people around here, I'm expecting to be fired any day. I just want to make it easy to go when that day finally comes."

At first I thought it was a joke. So I chuckled and then looked at him expecting him to continue with the "real" answer. But Walter just sat there, deadpan. Then in a matter-of-fact-way he said: "It's good not to have too many personal things around that make you feel tied to the place. It's work." It was clear he meant exactly what he said.

It was one of those big, "aha" moments you get in your professional career—a moment of total clarity. I was already a believer in not taking on more than could be really done. I understood the importance of standing firm on scope and expectation management. (I learned that the hard way from over-committing to clients and getting burned.) I had observed successful IT leaders push back on their colleagues who came with wish lists and project demands that didn't make sense for the business. But I never quite heard it said like this. And I certainly never saw anyone internalize this discipline and approach to such a degree that they would ready themselves for dismissal at a moment's notice.[5]

Manage Transitions

Warner Burke, an organizational development expert from Columbia University, states, "If you look at change efforts in organizations around the United States, you will see that 70 percent of these efforts fail." He also argues that 50 percent of leaders fail. These poor performance statistics are a result of poor organizational cultures and a lack of effective leadership.

We are creatures of habit, as innovation expert Arthur VanGundy likes to note. We sometimes resist change just because it is change. It's easier to stay within our comfort zones.[6]

One of the most important aspects of a large enterprise system implementation is to help people transition to the new ways of conducting business through the new system. In this section, I will describe the strategies that have helped me overcome this enormous challenge.

It isn't the changes that do you in, it's the transitions. They aren't the same thing. *Change* is situational: the move to a new site, the retirement of the founder, the reorganization of the roles on the team, or the revisions to the pension plan. *Transition*, in contrast, is psychological;

it is a process that people go through as they internalize and come to terms with the details that the change brings about.

In *Managing Transitions*, William Bridges explained that "it isn't the changes themselves that people resist. It's the losses and endings they have experienced and the transition they are resisting."[7] Bridges offered the following process for managing transitions:

- Identify who's losing what.
- Accept the reality and importance of the subjective losses.
- Don't be surprised by overreaction.
- Acknowledge the losses openly and sympathetically.
- Expect and accept the signs of grieving.
- Compensate for the losses.
- Give people information, and do it again and again.
- Define what's over and what isn't.
- Mark the endings.
- Treat the past with respect.
- Let people take a piece of the old way with them.
- Show how endings ensure the continuity of what really matters.

| It isn't the changes that do you in, it's the transitions.

I also suggest forming a transition management subteam to focus on the process. Include people in IT as well as in the division as part of the team. If you leave these important tasks to the project manager to handle, you are doomed. Project managers have enough on their plate: managing the work plan, coordinating meetings, leading the discovery and implementing phases, and so on. Because they have limited time, they will kick this can down the road until it's too late, or at best they'll make a modest attempt to manage change without material success.

Measure Benefits

Although elaborate systems are in place to show how IT budgets and spends capital, few systems are in place to demonstrate the return on that investment. In other words, although companies are managing IT spending, they are not managing IT returns. In terms of personal financing, it's akin to never holding your investment broker accountable for the performance of the portfolio. So it strikes me as counterintuitive that many IT leaders don't take the time to document a formal business case before a project. If you don't have a business case, you cannot measure the results. Maybe some leaders prefer not to be measured.

Some company cultures are not big on defining how to measure the results of technology-enabled business initiatives. In these cases, it is still helpful for the CIO to tell the story of how the new system created business value. Ken Harris, the CIO of Shaklee, explains it this way:

> Most of your business partners are happy to ask for new systems, but not as interested in defining how the success of new systems will be measured. Despite the lack of enthusiasm in the business for defining measurements, a good CIO is able to identify the intended business outcomes of a project and tell the story. For instance, our orders moved from a ratio of 70:30 call center to Web to 60:40 call center to Web. The ability to translate success in business terms can mean the difference between being viewed as an IT guy versus a business leader.

Although elaborate systems are in place to show how IT budgets and spends capital, few systems are in place to demonstrate the return on that investment.

Chapter 3 described how to write an effective business case. I hope you found value in the method described and will be able to use it to pitch your next project.

The final and most important activity after launching a new system (besides supporting it) is value management. Value management reinforces accountability for realizing the tangible business value by reviewing projections, ascertaining commitments, and monitoring results. This is a critical component of demand management, given that more than 40 percent of business and IT leaders view the return on investment (ROI) from technology-enabled investments as "marginal" or, even worse, view technology as a cost and a risk to be managed.[8]

IT departments are generally very good at describing the costs of a project but not as good at measuring business benefits. Standardizing and accelerating business processes and providing improved transparency for operations are essential to improving business execution, which in turn supports the organizational goals of revenue and profit growth.

Much research has been performed in this area. In the Blackwell Science *Information Systems Journal*, Shari Shang and Peter B. Seddon described the following benefits framework for enterprise systems:

Operational

- Cost reduction
- Cycle-time reduction
- Productivity improvement
- Quality improvement
- Customer-service improvement

Managerial

- Better resource management
- Improved decision making and planning
- Performance improvement

Strategic

- Support for business growth
- Support for a business alliance
- Business innovations
- Cost leadership
- Product differentiation
- External linkages

IT infrastructure

- Business flexibility for current and future changes
- IT cost reduction
- Increased IT infrastructure capability

Organizational

- Change in work patterns
- Organizational learning
- Empowerment
- Common vision[9]

The average small-business ERP implementation takes ten months, even though the installation work continues long after the go-live date hits, according to a recent Aberdeen Group survey data of 920 small businesses. The financial costs can be just as significant: Small businesses with less than $50 million in annual revenue will typically pay nearly $300,000 for ERP software and services, while larger businesses (those with revenues of $100 million to $250 million) will spend $1.4 million, the survey data states.

"Given this level of investment, one would think ROI would be top of mind for most companies," Cindy Jutras, the vice president and research fellow at Aberdeen, wrote in a March 2009 report. But it's not. The data show that 52 percent of respondents "sometimes" or "never" estimate ROI in order to cost-justify an ERP project (48 percent "always" do). And 75 percent "sometimes" or "never" measure ROI after the completion of ERP projects (just 25 percent "always" do).[10]

Failing to document and measure the benefits of an enterprise system implementation prevents you from understanding the value of the project and whether it is even aligned with the company's goals and objectives. It also prevents you from measuring whether end users are complying with the standard policies and processes, since these maxims are typically derived from the business case. But Greg Fell, the CIO of Terex Corporation, offers a caution:

> *Attempting to measure business benefits after the fact can be a significant overhead. It takes companies several years to realize the return on the investment of a large-scale enterprise system initiative. During that time, the business may undergo change that impacts the assumptions made in the original business case, which makes the benefits extremely difficult to measure. You could find yourself in a rabbit hole where you're spending more time and money trying to identify the benefits than the benefits are actually worth. You are better off focusing on a handful of key metrics rather than a litany of volatile measurements.*

An enterprise system implementation can offer a source of long-term savings, revenue generation, operational efficiencies, and even customer satisfaction. So be sure to dust off the business case created at the launch of the system, if you have one, and start measuring and reporting the realized value of the investment. But be careful of overanalyzing the data by agreeing with your business partners up front on the handful of key measurements of the value of the initiative.

Communicate IT Value

I am sure you would like to think that if you do a good job, people will notice and even thank you once in a while. The trouble is that part of a CIO's role is to make sure problems don't occur, so if you are doing a good job, people don't tend to notice it—or you. When was the last time you called your local cable company and thanked it for bringing you Internet access? When was the last time your department was credited for consistently delivering more value for less money? Being unnoticed is very dangerous, especially in an era of cost cutting.

IT marketing is about *leading* expectations with your business partners and communicating progress with goals and objectives. The challenge is that IT is often perceived as a high-cost, low-value provider of services. This is a result of ineffective attempts to convey the value of IT products and services.

> IT marketing is about *leading* expectations with your business partners and communicating progress with goals and objectives.

In *Unleashing the Power of IT: Bringing People, Business, and Technology Together*, Dan Roberts explained that marketing is one of the most important business disciplines:

> The formulation of the IT organization's image as "service provider of choice" is one of the most important factors for a successful IT cultural transformation. By and large our clients don't understand what we do. We need to market internally to have a shot at increasing our credibility, building partnerships, and turning around any negative perceptions. We live in a world in which perception matters, and this is particularly true for internal IT organizations in today's business world. If clients perceive us as mere code changers, network fixers,

and PC installers, how will they react when IT tries to move into a more strategic role in the organization?

In other cases, IT damages its own image and reputation by projecting an arrogant air that says, "We know what's best for the business because we're the technical experts." This looks even worse when the organization hasn't taken the time to explain how technology can be a strategic advantage to the business. Meanwhile, IT is competing with external outsourcers, consultants, vendors, and system integrators, which are very adept at getting in front of executive-level decision makers to convince them of the business benefits their companies can provide.

All these reasons explain why IT needs to market internally—to have a shot at increasing its credibility, building partnerships, and turning around any negative perceptions.

It's not about hype and empty promises; it's about creating an awareness of IT's value. It's about changing client perceptions by presenting a clear, consistent message about the value of IT. After all, if you don't market yourself, someone else will, and you might not like the image you end up with.[11]

Why are IT leaders generally bad at promoting their departments? Perhaps it's our introverted nature or that we have been so beaten down over the decades that we actually believe we are not worthy of such equivalence. Rubbish! Anyone who has achieved the CIO title cannot be *that* introverted. We must have successfully demonstrated our value to company executives at some point in our career, or we wouldn't be in our current role. We are also known to be highly analytical people, so why not leverage that strength to help communicate your department's successes? Begin by methodically listing your department's successes over the last quarter and its plans for the next quarter. As technology becomes more and more intertwined with business processes, we have a tremendous opportunity to exploit how we are a vital entity in our companies.

Create a Communication Program

After you have taken a moment to contemplate the achievements and initiatives that will help you promote your department, you are ready to begin considering ways to best market the value of IT to your business partners. It is important to understand that communication happens at all levels within IT, not just with the CIO, although the CIO certainly sets the tone and helps create the communication channels.

While it is desirable for communication to naturally flow throughout the organization, you will benefit from creating a structured communication program. A communication program helps you to define your audience, your key messages, and the frequency of your communications. If you're fortunate enough to have the budget, consider hiring a full-time communication specialist. Otherwise, you will need to identify someone in your department to assist you with the communication program part-time.

Define Your Audience

In every organization, there are many different audiences that an IT department needs to address. Obviously, you will need to fine-tune your communication program accordingly. By carefully thinking through your communication strategy and defining your plan, you can improve your relationship with your audience and the image of IT in your organization and perhaps your industry. It starts with positioning IT as a true *partner* to other business functions and transitioning away from being viewed as a mere service provider. It's easier said than done, and actions clearly speak louder than words.

There are nine main categories of stakeholders you should consider: the entire organization, functional areas, the IT department, presidents and department heads, board members, technology partners, business suppliers, customers, and job applicants. The following sections describe strategies for each audience type.

Audience 1: The Entire Organization. Let's start with your broadest audience: the entire organization. You need to communicate to everyone in your company, not just the department heads. In fact, it's a good idea to send a welcome e-mail to every employee who joins your company.

It is likely that your help desk already sends some sort of e-mail to new employees once they have been set up with a network account.

Why not add to the message and describe your department's vision, mission, and goals? It doesn't cost you anything, and it helps you make a great first impression with all of the new employees. And you know what they say about first impressions. In addition, I like to personally call new leaders in the organization to introduce myself and describe the products and services that IT provides. I find that the phone call goes a long way in building a solid relationship.

On a periodic basis, send all company employees updates on the happenings in IT—quarterly newsletters and scorecards typically work well. This group is diverse, so your messages should cover a broad set of topics. You can personalize the messages by embedding hyperlinks to help each employee get to content that is specific to his or her department (e.g., purchasing or marketing). A sample of a scorecard template is available on the companion website.

If you really want to be sophisticated, consider creating an annual report for IT that summarizes the achievements of the previous year and the plans for the upcoming year. I have made it a routine to create annual reports—with a lot of help from my team—and it has helped to convey a level of sophistication and maturity with IT. It also demonstrates that we are carefully measuring our performance and being very transparent about it. Annual reports also serve as an excellent reference guide for when you need to compare the performance of your department year after year.

It's a good practice to invite feedback from the organization through this correspondence, because you want to foster engagement and avoid coming across as selling or promoting your department.

Audience 2: Functional Areas. While the types of correspondence mentioned earlier allow you to communicate and engage a wide audience, it doesn't replace the personal touch of interactive meetings with functional areas. Ask the other department heads if they could let you attend their next staff meetings to give a short talk. Ironically, many department heads struggle with coming up with content for their staff meetings or don't enjoy speaking in front of a large audience (even if it's their own staff), so they will often jump at your offer to present.

Always grab every chance to get in front of as many people as possible in your organization. It is a wonderful opportunity to share achievements and current initiatives. More important, it is a great opportunity to answer questions and address any hot-button issues on their minds. Be sure to customize your message for the specific audience. If you are speaking to the sales and marketing department, talk about how your team is adding value to sales and marketing; avoid talking about accounting projects unless you want their eyes to roll back in their heads.

According to Tony Alessandra and Phillip L. Hunsaker, the authors of *Presentation Power*, "The more time you devote to analyzing your audience beforehand, the less you will have to do on the spot." Here is their advice on how you can acquire information in advance about your audience:

1.   Ask the presentation host for information about the audience. Find out general demographics such as age, sex, professional level, specific interests, and needs. Also ask what the group has responded well to in the past. What presentation styles were well received?

2.   Talk to members of the audience. If possible, arrive early enough to survey one or more members of the audience to find out what they expect and what they would like to hear about.

3.   Talk to other speakers. If you know other speakers who have spoken to the same group, ask them what worked and what they would do differently with the group.[12]

Here are some questions you should always ask yourself to help you to analyze the needs of each particular audience you will address:

- Why should these people listen to you?
- How does what you say affect them?
- What's in it for them to listen to you?
- Why is it important for the audience to hear what you have to say?

Always grab every chance to get in front of as many people as possible in your organization. It is a wonderful opportunity to share achievements and current initiatives.

Audience 3: The IT Department. Obviously, you need to communicate well with your own department so that your staff is aligned with the vision, mission, goals, and objectives of the department. People want to understand how they fit into the big picture. So start by working with your team to create departmental goals and cascade those goals to every member in your department. After you cascade your goals to your direct reports, they should add their specific objectives, designed to meet your goals, and cascade them to their staffs. At the end of the exercise, everyone in the department has a set of goals and objectives that are aligned with the department's vision. By performing this exercise, your staff will understand how they are contributing to the success of the department as well as the overall company.

Once performance objectives are in place for every employee, you can use your staff meetings to share achievements and plans for each of the goals. Employees enjoy seeing their projects up on the slides and are proud that they are part of the bigger picture. Use your staff meetings to publicly recognize employees for their efforts.

Depending on the size and location of your staff, you can also use written communications to update your staff on departmental initiatives. Staff meetings are generally better for your staff, though, because you can open up the floor and address people's questions and concerns. It also gives you an opportunity to involve others in presenting their projects.

Audience 4: Presidents and Department Heads. Presidents and department heads represent another category of business partners whom you need to communicate with on a periodic basis. The medium and frequency of communication with this group greatly depends on the size and location of the company. Ideally, in-person meetings work best with these VIPs, so get on their calendars on a recurring basis. These stakeholders are not likely to read—or even peruse—your scorecards and newsletters. Most executives are extremely busy, and your written communications will end up on the bottom of their reading lists. That being said, very short e-mails—the type that can be conveniently read on a smartphone—that demonstrate how IT successes are tied to business value can be a potent form of communicating with presidents and departments heads.

For tips on communicating with presidents and department heads, I turned to executive recruiters who spend time with these stakeholders when recruiting new CIOs. Rich Brennen, a partner at Spencer Stuart, describes the best practices when communicating with chief officers of all types (CXOs):

> *The biggest mistake a CIO can make when speaking with another CXO is focusing the discussion on the IT agenda rather on the business agenda. The CIO needs to put himself in the CXO's shoes because his job is to enable the CXO's agenda.*
>
> *There are demands placed on CIOs from virtually every function in the company, so it's important for CIOs to spearhead a companywide project prioritization effort. Each function head naturally believes their priorities should be the top priorities for the CIO. The project prioritization effort allows everyone to weigh in and ultimately align on the top priorities for the company and for IT.*
>
> *CIOs need to learn how each CXO likes to communicate: some prefer informal discussion, others like to be informed based on project milestones, and others like recurring update meetings. As a CIO, you can't enforce your style on them. You're the supplier. You need to treat the CXOs the same way you want to be treated by your technology suppliers.*
>
> *You also have to make a great first impression. It's a cruel world, and there aren't a lot of second chances, so if you botch your first meeting, you may not get a second chance. And, most important, once you do get everyone aligned on the priorities, you have to deliver.*

Audience 5: Board Members. IT leaders are often expected to provide updates to the company's board of directors. CIOs can use these opportunities to communicate achievements, current initiatives, and issues in driving business outcomes.

Phil Schneidermeyer is a partner at Heidrick & Struggles, a global executive search and leadership consulting firm. I met with Phil recently and asked him to describe how IT leaders can improve their communication with executive boards. Here's his reply:

> *When preparing to speak to the board, it's important to do your homework. You should learn the backgrounds of each board member. What's their day job? What other boards do they sit on? What is their knowledge and interest in the topics you will be presenting? Also, it's equally important to understand the communication style of your board. Do they prefer that*

executives file in one after another and present slides, or are they interested in a dialogue? Spending a little time up front to do some research will pay dividends for you and your team.

Spencer Stuart's Brennen puts it this way:

The board is a collection of individuals with a variety of backgrounds and interests. Some members really care about IT; others care less about IT or may even be afraid of it. Some board members don't have a lot of understanding of IT, and some have considerable knowledge. When you are talking to the board, you are not talking to a group of ten people; you are talking to ten individuals. Out of a group of ten board members, there are usually at least three who really matter: the three the rest of the members look to as the IT thought leaders on the board.

So do your homework to discover the three members who matter the most. If a board member happens to be a CEO of another company, contact the CIO at the company to find out how the CEO views IT. By identifying the IT opinion leaders on the board, you will be able to tailor your message to these individuals and accomplish much more.

Also, you really need to understand the company's strategy and performance before entering the boardroom. How is the board feeling about the company? What are the issues they are discussing? Having the answers to these questions allows you to understand the tenor of the room. The way to get this information is by talking to others who meet with the board on a regular basis, including the CEO.

Since IT is a mystery to many board members, you need to talk about the impact of what you are doing and its relationship to the business strategy. So, if you are asking for approval to spend money, always discuss it in terms of an investment. For instance, let's say you learn the company is focused on acquisitions and you're about to pitch a business case to spend $50 million to build a data center. Position the proposal as an investment, allowing the company the capacity to grow and facilitate the integration of acquisitions. Always present to the board in the context of business outcomes, not IT outcomes.

Out of a group of ten board members, there are usually at least three who really matter: the three the rest of the members look to as the IT thought leaders on the board.

—Rich Brennen, partner at Spencer Stuart

Audience 6: Technology Partners. Technology partners represent another category of stakeholders to communicate with on a regular basis. IT functional owners are usually assigned to technology partners and act as relationship managers. You may want to consider inviting your key partners to your IT management meetings, or even staff meetings, where they can present their new products and roadmaps. This topic is discussed further in Chapter 5.

Audience 7: Business Suppliers. If you are involved in SCM, you are already meeting with your company's suppliers. If you're not meeting with your suppliers, get them on your communication radar. The stronger your relationships with this group, the more opportunity you will have to help the company streamline operations and reduce costs. Some companies use newsletters to communicate with their business suppliers. If this is the case with your company, be sure to get a column in the newsletter and have someone on your team write articles that are relevant to the business suppliers.

Audience 8: Customers. Customers are certainly another critical stakeholder to consider when defining your communication plan. Your ability to communicate with your customers varies dramatically by industry. For instance, if you're a supplier to retailers such as Walmart, you generally have the opportunity to meet with your customers to discuss supply chain topics. If your customers are consumers, however, the chances of you having direct contact with them is limited at best, even though you may have technology in place that they use to interact with your company (e.g., a company website or portal).

Still, with a little thought and creativity, there are ways to get pertinent messages across to your customers. Your company is very likely to be already leveraging social media (e.g., Facebook and Twitter) to interact with customers. This is a great medium for you to convey how your company is using business technology to enrich the customer experience—and also to invite feedback.

Audience 9: Job Applicants. Many prospective employees are interested in understanding the technology that is available at the company.

If your company is using social media such as Facebook, consider using that medium to highlight the technologies in use at your company. Some companies create brochures for their IT departments to attract both IT candidates and non-IT candidates. The career page on your company's website is also an excellent medium to market how IT is being used.

A CIO Roundtable

On a similar note, you can benefit from establishing a CIO roundtable with the employees in your department as well as across the organization. Again, you need to carefully consider the interests and concerns of your audience.

I suggest that you have these meetings over breakfast or lunch (food always makes people happy) and that you include no more than 10 people, which makes it more interactive. While the roundtables are a great opportunity for you to share information, they represent an excellent forum for you to *listen* to your audience to gain important feedback. You can get your best ideas from roundtables with people from different functions. To get your feet wet, start with having these sessions with just a functional area that you are most familiar with and expand from there.

I asked Richard Lattmann, the associate vice president of U.S. infrastructure services at Sanofi, how he and his organization go about collecting feedback from the users. Here is what he told me:

> *While we survey our internal customers to get their perspective on our services, we tend to get more value from having roundtable discussions with our customers. We call these discussions "Voice of the Customer." These sessions are very helpful because they tend to transition from a discussion on satisfaction with solving service tickets to shedding light on new opportunities where IT can add value to the business.*

Some organizations form governing bodies to define standard processes and prioritize projects. Communicating effectively with these groups is critical because they are your champions and ambassadors to the rest of the organization. Customarily, IT functional owners (relationship managers) will participate in these committees to align IT resources with business priorities. It is very important that minutes from these meetings are disseminated to other stakeholders in the function or even throughout the company to build awareness of the priorities. Consider summarizing the key decisions and priorities and including the information in your IT scorecards (e.g., the top 10 priorities for purchasing or accounting).

Go Global with Applications

Today, more and more international companies are moving toward global enterprise systems as a result of mergers and acquisitions and the expansion of their global presence. These global efforts are providing unprecedented opportunities to standardize and optimize business processes. This section describes the benefits and the challenges of standardizing business processes and technologies on an international level.

Benefits

The basic purpose of an information system is the provision of information to support decision making. The improved flow of information provides companies with the ability to better coordinate and manage their operations while also providing increased visibility to their global supply chains. Traditionally, this flow of information has been hindered because of a number of factors, including technological infrastructure, poor and disparate systems, and lack of standardization.

Most international companies have operated in a relatively autonomous nature from country to country, and the supporting IT has been managed and developed in a similar way. However, many companies are realizing the importance of a global operation having a centrally managed and coordinated IT infrastructure. Accordingly, companies' developing IT strategies to facilitate their global operations has resulted in the emergence of global enterprise systems that contribute to achieving business strategy.

In his case study "Implementing ERP Systems Globally," Paul Hawking lists the following drivers for global IT applications:

- **Global consumer or customer.** Corporate customers have operations in numerous locations or due to consumers' mobility, access to centralized systems is required. This would be relevant in airline, credit card, and accommodation-related companies.
- **Global product.** IT infrastructure supports the sales of the same product in numerous locations, or the products and/or their components are produced via subsidiaries across the world.
- **Rationalized operations.** Subsidiaries are located to take advantage of local opportunities, where increased coordination and control is required.
- **Flexible operations.** Due to local opportunities, operations are moved from location to location. This is facilitated by standardized IT infrastructure.
- **Joint resources.** Shared services enable subsidiaries to standardize business practices and gain efficiencies through shared resources such as personnel and facilities.
- **Duplicate facilities.** Companies duplicate facilities in different locations including the IS infrastructure, to standardize practices and improve coordination and control by management.
- **Scarce resources.** IT infrastructure can facilitate the sharing of scarce resources and expertise across international boundaries.
- **Risk reduction.** Access to relevant information related to global operations in relation to supply chain management, currency conversion, global markets, and business partners can alleviate possible risks.
- **Legal requirements.** Legislated information requirements in one or more countries can be consolidated.
- **Economies of scale for systems.** IT infrastructure through the standardization and consolidation of business processes can facilitate the reduction in IT systems and supporting personnel.[13]

Researchers believe that the growth in the number of global enterprise system implementations is a result of several factors:

- The need to streamline and improve business processes.
- The growing desire to better manage information systems expenditure.

- Competitive pressures to become a low-cost producer.
- Increased responsiveness to customers and their needs.
- The need to integrate business processes.
- The ability to provide a common platform and better data visibility.
- The fact that global enterprise systems are becoming a strategic tool for the move toward a digital business.[14]

Challenges

Global enterprise systems can fail for the reasons mentioned earlier in this chapter, but, global transformations add an extra layer of challenges to consider. These include operational differences, language, currency, number of application instances, culture, laws, unions, time zones, costs, funding, availability of IT staff, and governance.

While working on a project to standardize business processes at a company headquartered in Germany, I discovered the organizational structure to be very lean and the approach to problem solving more methodical than what I had experienced in the United States. Having just worked at an online startup based in the United States, I had to take time to adjust my work style in order to be successful in my new role. Instead of sitting down with a fellow business leader and simply talking about the pros and cons of a potential solution to a problem, I now needed to write down my thoughts in a very comprehensive and cohesive way to demonstrate that I had thought out the situation, identified all of the alternatives, and weighed all of the pros and cons before reaching my decision proposal.

This is not to say that some U.S.-based companies don't also prefer this approach, but this German-based company certainly expected a very disciplined and meticulous approach to problem solving. You may recall the story I told earlier, from Jeff Boyd of Operation Explore, about how a team member from Japan didn't want to put things in writing. That project also involved partnering with team members from Germany, so you can imagine the complexity of the communications.

Let's delve a bit further into three issues that tend to get a lot of airtime when it comes to global implementations: costs, culture, and governance.

Costs. There is much debate about whether a single international implementation costs more than a domestic project. Some argue that an international project costs as much as 20 percent more than a local project. Global ERP execution involves additional expenses compared to domestic rollouts. Aspects involving higher costs include travel, training, documentation translations, purchase of additional ERP modules to accommodate local tax laws, upgraded telecommunications infrastructures, and additional consultants, who charge higher fees in some less-developed countries.

Others believe the costs are relative to regional costs and that the global support involved in international implementation actually lowers implementation costs. From my perspective, costs can be controlled based on how well you plan and execute the project, and it's less dependent on the location of your sites. All sites incur costs with an enterprise system implementation, even if they go with a stand-alone solution.

Even higher travel costs can be considered and dealt with in advance. Instead of traveling to the remote sites, you can instill the practice of video conferencing and significantly reduce costs. While it's usually important to meet an important stakeholder for the first time in person, subsequent meetings can be conducted by video conference, webinar, or teleconference.

Training services can also usually drive up costs significantly, but they can be reduced with webinars and e-learning. Of course, there are times when in-person meetings are necessary. In those cases, project managers can be very selective about who really needs to travel and who could be on video or on the phone. The point is that you need to challenge current thinking and be creative about how to keep your costs low even though the implementation site may be many thousands of miles away.

Culture. The implementation of a global enterprise system is often met with cultural issues that must be addressed up front. The cultural issues come in many forms, such as societal or organizational, and it's imperative that a project team take on a global mind-set so it can appreciate the cultural differences that can deter the success of the project.

In most global enterprise system implementations, the initiation, decision, and selection stages are usually dominated by the parent country and may reflect a desire for more control and standardization of the work processes. Thus, the new system is imposed "top-down" in most countries, turning this process into a deterministic one, with no leeway for local effect related to structural and cultural adjustment.[15]

The more sophisticated and collaborative organizations work to embrace the other countries in the initiation, decision, and selection stages. They recognize that a command-and-control approach to global system rollouts will alienate the intended users and lead to resistance and even project failure.

Even when organizations take a more democratic style with global system rollouts, they tend to overlook the cultural issues, which can also lead to a poor outcome. Let's examine some strategies with culture in multinational system rollouts.

Culture is often symbolized as an iceberg or an onion, to represent its visible and invisible aspects. The visible components—also called practices—are manifested by symbols (words, gestures, pictures, and objects), heroes (real or imaginary people serving as good models of behavior), and rituals (collective activities without a practical purpose but essential to keep the individual within the collective norms). You can observe all of these manifestations when you visit other countries and when you receive foreign visitors. However, only the insiders of those cultures can easily capture their real meaning.

In *Global Project Management: Communication, Collaboration and Management across Borders*, Jean Binder described the following activities when managing projects abroad:

- Discover the meanings of different symbols used by local people, in order to respect and follow their basic instructions. In project management, the symbols can translate into the specialized terms, techniques and diagrams;
- Know their local heroes, to understand the role models of behavior. The organizational heroes can be the people who advance quickly in their career, employees receiving management awards or popular team members;
- Understand and respect the rituals, which in business are often present in the way people organize or attend meetings, in local practices for celebrating success, negotiation processes and by the demonstration of power when attending or rejecting meeting invitations.

The "invisible" core of culture is formed by the values, which broadly represent tendencies and preferences over different aspects of social or professional life. These are some examples of values that may affect global projects, as they differ depending on the geographical location of team members:

- Is it polite to decline meetings because they occur during your lunch hour? Conversely, is it acceptable to book regular meetings during the lunch hour? Is it acceptable to organize a meeting starting at 6 P.M. on a summer Friday afternoon?
- Is it acceptable to request your project team to cancel their summer holidays to finish a late deliverable?
- Are project managers more effective when they use their formal power (their hierarchical position) or their expert power (based on their competences)?
- What is the preferred leadership style for project managers, in each part of the project life cycle?
- How important is the performance of the team members compared to the way they respect and relate to their colleagues?[16]

Doing some homework up front by reading books and other forms of literature on the countries you are planning to implement in will go a long way toward helping you and your organization to be successful. At the very least, it will demonstrate to your colleagues in the other countries that you are attempting to understand and respect their cultures.

Governance.   As challenging as it is to create and maintain an effective governance program in a single country, it gets even more difficult when you have to put a framework around how decisions are made at a global level. This section discusses the various forms of governance that companies can consider, based on their needs.

In Chapter 3, I described the components of a governance framework. All of what was described in the framework can be applied to global implementations. The major difference, however, is the level of autonomy you want to offer the individual countries. That is, if individual countries are going to have a separate instance of the enterprise system, you may want to consider replicating the governance framework in each country and have each instance work relatively independently. But that approach hampers your ability to create and enforce standardized business practices throughout the company.

If, however, you have a single instance of the system, the best approach would be to have a single instance of the governance framework composed of representatives from each of the countries. For instance, the purchasing process leadership committee could be made up of individuals from each country or from a region, such as Europe.

When the organizational structure is not aligned with the transformation objectives of an enterprise system rollout, the path back to the old ways of operating is hard to resist. End-to-end global process owners are instrumental for successful and sustainable change. Without global process owners, decision making becomes time and resource intensive—and ultimately ineffective. For that reason, up-front agreement on the priorities and expected outcomes of the transformation among business areas must be achieved. Clear attention should be given to qualitative and long-term objectives as well—for example, sustaining common processes to enable faster mergers and acquisitions in the future. To better assess your governance requirements, consider the following governance readiness criteria:

- How does your organization make decisions?
- Who has decision rights?
- What is the breadth of the decision rights?
- How will accountability be assigned—by function, country, or other means?

If the business runs more locally than globally, setting up a "global process owners'" structure (such as the governance framework previously discussed) and performance measurements will allow for clear decision making as new global processes are being designed. Consider the following criteria for assessing the performance of global process management:

- Are the performance (business and process) measurements defined globally, or does each country or business have its own definitions?
- How far do you want to drive global performance indicators? For instance, a manufacturing company that wants to make global

manufacturing decisions needs to have a common definition of costs of goods sold.

Go Global with Infrastructure

Technology has enabled businesses to become highly distributed. Whether *distributed* means across a region, across a country, or around the globe, one thing is certain: Headquarters isn't where all of the action is. With about two-thirds of the workforce operating in locations other than headquarters, and with an estimated 450 million mobile workers around the world, businesses now operate everywhere all of the time.[17]

Business today has no borders. Despite the global economic uncertainty, companies are expanding all over the world. Leading international businesses are rewarded for their flexibility and long-term outlook in the face of short-term uncertainty. The opportunities to grow and expand internationally are boundless, and IT leaders need to put on a global headset to help their companies extend their reach by planning and executing a worldwide technology infrastructure platform.

Christine L. Borgman, author of *From Gutenberg to the Global Information Infrastructure: Access to Information in the Networked World*, wrote the following:

> The creation of a successful GII [global information infrastructure] could have as much impact on global culture as Gutenberg's printing press has done since its development in the mid-fifteenth century. The GII is expected to revolutionize the ease with which electronic information can be shared across the planet much as the printing press enabled an abundance of printed information to become easily accessible for anyone who knew how to read.[18]

The globalization of businesses has created challenges and opportunities for organizations. Do you keep a federated IT model in which each country essentially runs its own infrastructure, or do you centralize operations by leveraging private and public cloud infrastructure? Do you try to do both, with a hybrid model? These are the questions CIOs are asking themselves, their teams, and their technology partners.

For many rapidly growing businesses with limited international experience, these global opportunities often present major challenges. For IT leaders, doing business internationally literally means taking on a whole new world of concerns.

Of course, cloud computing is revolutionizing the way organizations are delivering software, data, storage, and processing power to their employees, customers, and suppliers all over the world. Cloud computing is a break from the past by offering virtualization, democratization of computing, scalability, fast provisioning, and the commoditization of infrastructure. Although these areas have existed for some time, the recent trends toward combining them have resulted in a paradigm shift in computing, both domestically and internationally.

Choose the Right Number of Instances

The right number of instances for your enterprise system involves many variables and careful thought. The current number of instances you are running is usually a result of your organizational structure, your location, and perhaps mere happenstance. To make the right decision for your organization, you need to consider organizational structure and economies of scale. Based on your business, including your financial, competitive, geographic, structural, and forward-looking landscape, you can decide the relative importance of these factors.[19]

Top Plays

- One of the most significant pitfalls with enterprise system projects is the lack of effective teamwork.
- A team-building program can help the members to begin to trust one another.
- The discover phase captures current business processes and readiness for a conversion.
- Enterprise system implementations help companies to align business units with company policies and processes to realize the benefits of a common operating platform.

(continued)

- The develop-and-implement phase of an enterprise system roll-out is focused on design, development, conversion, testing, and support.
- Say no so you can focus on the critical activities.
- Build a transition management team.
- Value management reinforces accountability for realizing tangible business value.
- IT marketing helps you *lead* expectations with your business partners and communicate progress.
- Globalizing systems leads to process improvements, better IT cost management, and improved responsiveness to customers.

Notes

1. Michael Krigsman, "2011 ERP Survey: New IT Failure Research and Statistics," ZDNet, March 1, 2011, http://www.zdnet.com/blog/project failures/2011-erp-survey-new-it-failure-research-and-statistics/12486.
2. *Ibid.*
3. Patrick Lencioni, *The Five Dysfunctions of a Team: A Leadership Fable* (San Francisco: Jossey-Bass, 2002), 187–190.
4. David van Adelsberg and Edward A. van Adelsberg, *Trolley: Running Training Like a Business* (San Francisco: Berret-Koeler, 1999), x.
5. Marc J. Schiller, *The 11 Secrets of Highly Influential IT Leaders* (Mamaroneck, NY: privately printed, 2011), 71–72.
6. Arthur B. VanGundy, *Getting to Innovation: How Asking the Right Questions Generates the Great Ideas Your Company Needs* (New York: Amacom, 2007), 3.
7. William Bridges, *Managing Transitions: Making the Most of Change*, 2nd ed. (Cambridge, MA: privately printed, 2003), 42–68.
8. Nicholas Carr, "IT Doesn't Matter," *Harvard Business Review*, May 1, 2003, 41–49.
9. Shari Shang and Peter B. Seddon, "Assessing and Managing the Benefits of Enterprise Systems: The Business Manager's Perspective," *Information Systems Journal*, 2002, 271–277.
10. Thomas Wailgum, "SMB ERP Projects: Don't Forget the ROI," *CIO*, April 1, 2009, http://www.cio.com/article/487794/SMB_ERP_Projects_Don_t_Forget_the_ROI.

11. Dan Roberts, *Unleashing the Power of IT: Bringing People, Business, and Technology Together* (Hoboken, NJ: John Wiley & Sons, 2011), 140.

12. Tony Alessandra and Phillip L. Hunsaker, *Presentation Power* (Carlsbad, CA: privately printed, 2005), 175.

13. Paul Hawking, "Implementing ERP Systems Globally: A Case Study." *International Journal of Strategic Information Technology and Applications* 1, no. 3 (2010): 22–23

14. *Ibid.*

15. Esther Brainin, "Experiences of Cultures in Global ERP Implementation," *IGI Global*, 2008, 175.

16. Jean Binder, *Global Project Management: Communication, Collaboration and Management across Borders* (Farnham, UK: Gower, 2007), 24–25.

17. Riverbed Technology, *The CIO's New Guide to Design of Global IT Infrastructure* (San Francisco: privately printed, 2011), 1.

18. Christine L. Borgman, *From Gutenberg to the Global Information Infrastructure: Access to Information in the Networked World* (London: MIT Press, 2003), 1.

19. Oracle, *Choosing the Number of Instances for JD Edwards EnterpriseOne* (Redwood Shores, CA: privately printed, 2007), 1–3.

Chapter 5

Step 5: Support

Care more than others think wise. Risk more than others think safe. Dream more than others think practical. Expect more than others think possible.

—Howard Schultz, CEO, Starbucks Coffee

Support: Provide superior services to maximize the return on investment in business technology.

IT support services are constantly being reshaped as long-established platforms are being replaced by those built on cloud services, mobile computing, and social networking. These transformative technologies are clearly making the transition from early adoption to mainstream adoption. They are also introducing complexity into the internal IT support model. But just because services are being moved to the cloud or to consumer devices doesn't mean IT should abrogate its responsibility to provide superior support services—the buck still stops with the CIO.

This chapter explains how to create a portfolio of services and set clear expectations with your technology partners and your end user community. While you will need to learn some new methods, they can typically be overlaid onto your existing support processes. Change can be difficult, but with a well-thought-out support program, IT can free itself of some of the nitty-gritty work of data center administration and focus on helping to enable business goals through the use of strategic technologies.

Create Service Level Agreements

Many IT departments pay lip service to establishing the measurements for support services. When they do create the measurements, they often just describe the services without providing any methods to evaluate them. It's worth taking the time to establish a comprehensive service level agreement (SLA) that describes the expected levels of service, how the services will be measured, and how IT will communicate the actual results. This chapter describes the major components of an SLA and how you can get started.

An SLA is a contract between the IT department and its users (i.e., employees in other departments within the company who use its products and services) that specifies, in measurable terms, the services and commitments that the IT department and related service providers will provide as well as the expectations and obligations of the user organization. The SLA incorporates performance measurements from contracts that you have with third-party providers so that you have one cohesive SLA for the company.

While meeting with Ken Murdoch, the CIO of Save the Children, I asked him how he sets expectations with his business on support services and how his strategy has helped him to improve service and satisfaction. This is what he told me:

> All of our support services are supported by agreed-upon service level agreements, not only for desk side support but for IT procurement. Our strategy and services are evaluated annually via survey, and we use the

response data to drive process improvements, increase staffing requests to address specific areas where complaints are registered, and [find] new ways to use innovation to address user requirements, training, and self-service.

We scale up or down our priority-one tickets based on crisis response and/or seasonality. If we are in emergency response mode, service and support to our responders takes the highest precedence and other support tickets are scaled down, and it is communicated to the end users at that time. The same takes place for month-end and year-end close and for our peak fundraising season, which is October through December.

As David Kaufman, the CIO of Aramark Corporation, puts it, "Service metrics, such as the average response time to internal help-desk tickets and system uptime, are now considered table stakes by most companies. CIOs need to solve these types of issues early on so they earn the confidence of the leadership team and be invited to partner on initiatives that drive business growth."

With that in mind, let's get you started with the topics covered in a typical SLA. An SLA does the following:

- Describes how users will be informed of all planned and unplanned infrastructure, application, or service outages, or changes.
- Explains the classification of help desk tickets in terms of their prioritization.
- Explains the coordination process for service degradation (e.g., system performance) or failure correction (e.g., bug fixes) and states how the user will be kept informed of the status.
- Describes what training services and materials will be provided to the user to minimize procedural errors.
- Provides details on backup and recovery services.
- Defines the expected system response time for key transactions.
- Describes the availability of systems and services.
- States the security methods to be used to protect all system resources from unauthorized access, monitoring, or tampering.
- Explains support model (e.g., tier 1, tier 2) and hours of operation.
- Provides user satisfaction survey results.
- Describes what performance data and analysis reports will be provided to the user organization to show service quality and the level of user support provided.

When authoring an SLA, consider including the following components:

- Support hours
- System uptime
- Issue classification
- Performance measurement
- Security maintenance
- End user satisfaction maintenance
- Service ticket response time management
- Communication of end user responsibilities

Support Hours

Providing the hours of coverage is a basic component of an SLA and should always be included. It helps IT set expectations for normal hours of support as well as for evenings, weekends, and holidays.

If you rely on third-party providers to support your applications and/or infrastructure products, you can use this section to communicate their hours of support. Again, this allows you to have one comprehensive document for all internally and externally provided services.

This section can also be used to delineate the services to be expected at different times. For instance, while all types of tickets are addressed during normal business hours, perhaps only production down tickets will be addressed in the evenings.

System Uptime

System uptime is a common measurement in SLAs and can be calculated several different ways, providing an excellent barometer on how well you are servicing your end users. Typical benchmarks include:

- Percentage of time that core business applications are expected to be up and running.
- Percentage of time that core infrastructure (e.g., e-mail, Internet, voice mail) is expected to be up and running.
- Percentage of time that *all* core systems are expected to be up and running.
- Number of expected system outages.

Issue Classification

The issue classification section defines the various types of priorities assigned to help desk tickets along with the measurements for collecting and closing all tickets. Operational issues are usually classified into three types of priorities: high, medium, and low. The differences among the classifications are typically as follows:

High: Loss of Service (Immediate Follow-Up)
- Availability of system (system down).
- Significant financial effect on business.
- Defect with critical functionality affecting large number of users.
- Integration issues that result in incorrect financial reporting.

Medium: Inconvenience (Prompt Follow-Up)
- Availability of component of a system, but a workaround is available.
- No financial effect on business.
- Defect with functionality affecting multiple users.
- Unusual latency and intermittent failing.

Low: Nuisance (Reasonable Follow-Up)
- Noncritical procedural questions.
- No financial effect on business.
- Defect affecting a single user.

Performance Measurement

Another component to measure in SLAs is performance time or transaction response time. This component involves up-front work to derive the standards for the measurements. As an example, 95 percent of the accounting transactions will be completed within three seconds, with no transactions exceeding seven seconds. Typical benchmarks include:

- Percentage of time that core business applications are expected to achieve performance measurements.
- Percentage of time that core infrastructure applications are expected to achieve performance measurements.
- Percentage of time that *all* core systems are expected to achieve performance measurements.

Security Maintenance

The measurement of compliance to security policies helps a company to assess various aspects of security. Typical benchmarks include:

- Percentage of users expected to be trained in the user security policy.
- Percentage of data expected to be backed up on a daily basis.
- Percentage of systems expected to be in compliance with security policy.
- Number of expected IT-related security incidents.
- Percentage of data expected to be restored from backup with required response time.
- Number of expected issues with segregation of duties.
- Expected response time to assign, change, and remove access privileges.

Maintain End User Satisfaction

SLAs should also provide benchmarking metrics for end user satisfaction. These metrics can be measured through periodic user surveys. Typical benchmark metrics include the level of expected satisfaction in the following categories:

- Ease of use
- Functionality
- Response time
- Reporting
- Support
- Training
- Business benefits

As described in Chapter 2, the benchmarking metrics along with *actual* results should be included in scorecards and published periodically to all users.

Service Ticket Response Time Management

Timely and effective response to IT user queries and problems requires a well-designed and well-executed service desk and incident management process.

John Levine, the global head of infrastructure at a major retailer, has developed SLAs to communicate the services being provided to each of the 873 stores in the United States and the 600 international stores.

"We review our performance to our SLAs every week during the year, and every day during the holiday shopping season," he says. "Our SLA review process helps us to understand our response time to user issues and hardware failure and replacement rates. We use the information to help make the necessary improvements so that our stores can operate effectively and efficiently."

Diane Montalto, the vice president of IT for a publicly traded pharmaceutical company, started with the company as an engineer 13 years ago and took over IT 3 years ago. Her department has come a long way in the last several years because of her relentless focus on quality and service. Here's how she explains it:

> Up until a few years ago, IT was viewed as a black hole. People made requests for IT services, and they wouldn't receive a timely response. We also had outsourcing arrangements that just weren't working. Since then we made significant progress with our services by focusing on four pillars: reliability, customer service, cost savings, and compliance. We have quarterly review meetings with key business stakeholders where we share progress on current projects, review service metrics, and openly discuss issues and business requirements. The meetings have helped us foster trust with our user community and create transparency with IT.

An effective service desk and incident management process includes setting up a service desk function with registration, incident escalation, trend and root cause analysis, and resolution. The business benefits include increased productivity through the quick resolution of user queries. In addition, an organization can address root causes (such as poor user training) through effective reporting. Typical benchmarks include:

- Percentage of tickets expected to be resolved on the first call.
- Percentage of tickets expected to be resolved within one working day, three working days, five working days, and so on.
- Percentage of calls expected to be abandoned.
- Percentage of tickets expected to be reopened.
- Average expected duration of call.

Whether or not you have outsourced your IT help desk, it is important to take time to analyze the data and try to identify patterns of behavior. For instance, are many users calling about the same issue over and over again? Is a particular division in your company struggling with a specific system or set of issues? Are most of your tickets related to questions, or do they have to do with software defects? Having this information in the form of an analytical report will help you create action plans to address the issues and reduce their recurrence.

Depending on the complexity of your shop, you may need many different types of analytical reports. Many IT departments categorize their tickets by tiers. For instance, tier 1 is your first line of defense for issues such as password resets or assistance with Microsoft Excel. A tier 2 ticket may be to grant access privileges to an accounting system. A tier 3 ticket may be related to a user having difficulty processing a journal entry in your enterprise system.

Now that we have that defined, let's look at some common reporting benchmarks:

- Number of tickets closed in the previous week by support tier (tier 1, tier 2, tier 3).
- Percentage of tickets closed.
- Response time to close the tickets. For instance, how many of the closed tickets were resolved within one day, two to three days, four to seven days, and so on? Show this in the form of a percentage as well.
- Beginning balance of open tickets for the current week.
- Number of tickets that were previously closed by IT and had to be reopened because the user was not satisfied.
- Currently aging tickets (one day old, two to three days old, four to seven days old, and so on).

It is helpful to report on these by tier as well as by the groups within each tier. For instance, in tier 3 you may have dozens of software applications or other technologies you want to collect data on.

The measurements described in the previous list only get you so far. They just tell you the *what* and not the *why*. Why are all of these people calling the help desk? What problems are they experiencing?

Can I deliver training or communicate information to help reduce the number of tickets?

To build an understanding of the *why*, you have to reach deeper into your help desk system and build a report based on reason codes. There are at least two types of reason codes to evaluate. The first is the symptom. A *symptom* is a feature or characteristic that is regarded as the indicating condition of a problem for a user. For instance, a symptom can be that a user forgot how to create a journal entry in the accounting system. The second reason code to consider is the resolution. A *resolution* indicates how you went about resolving the user's issue. In the previous example, the issue may have been resolved by training the user in how to create a journal entry. Here are some examples of reason codes:

Symptom
- Data issue
- Software defect
- New requirement for software change
- Question
- Performance issue
- Hardware issue
- Request for system access

Resolution
- Data repaired
- Defect identified and recorded in change management system
- New software request directed to governance process
- Training provided
- Performance issue resolved
- Hardware issue resolved
- System access request fulfilled

Reason codes provide a wealth of information to CIOs who are interested in reducing the number of service tickets and keeping users and IT personnel satisfied. Of course, being able to report on reason codes means that your staff has to record the reasons as they open and close tickets. That sounds easier than it sometimes is to achieve. It comes down to people understanding that the extra step is worth it because it will help reduce tickets and increase user satisfaction levels.

Once you establish the reason codes and get your staff to enter the codes in your help desk system on a routine basis, you are ready to report on the data and draw some valuable insights from it. One of the best ways to report on reason code data is to build a matrix with the resolution codes listed down the page and the symptom codes across the page.

When you launch this process, you may run into some data quality issues, such as IT staff coding tickets using the wrong reason codes. For example, a ticket with the reason code to request system access but the resolution code that training was provided is probably not correct. It will take some time to iron out the wrinkles, but the insight from the reporting is definitely worth it. Armed with a quantitative analysis of the symptoms that are causing the most tickets and work for your team, you can create action plans to address the root cause and increase productivity and satisfaction.

Communication of End User Responsibilities

In addition to defining the responsibilities and commitments of the IT department, it is equally important to identify what IT expects from its end users. Remember, this is a partnership! Here are some examples of expectations that IT can set for its users. Users shall:

- Direct all service requests to the help desk.
- Respond to help desk inquiries for additional information necessary to resolve the tickets.
- Become educated on and adhere to business policies and processes related to the systems.
- Ensure adequate segregation of duties when requesting application access.
- Participate in training.
- Ensure applicable access is removed when no longer required.

In summary, an SLA helps IT articulate the levels of services it delivers and how those services will be measured and communicated. These agreements further strengthen the partnership between IT and other departments in an organization. What matters most, however, is that you do what you say you are going to do.

Determine an Approach to IT Charge-Backs

An IT charge-back is a financial management strategy to describe how costs are incurred and recovered by IT in support of the business. This strategy contrasts with the traditional practice in which a centralized department absorbs all of the costs for hardware, software, telecom, and services, and those costs are treated simply as corporate overhead. This section addresses the major opportunities, considerations, approaches, and benefits for implementing an IT charge-back methodology.

Not all organizations favor an IT charge-back because they believe it just creates a lot of extra administrative work with little value to show for it. It also can be a deterrent in an organization's attempt to standardize on common platforms as business units push back on corporate allocations for the standard technologies. While IT charge-backs aren't for every organization, if you are considering charging your use community for IT services or want to improve on what you already have in place, this section should offer you some interesting points to consider.

Retail infrastructure head Levine believes that charge-backs can cause you to lose control of spending:

> If you start charging back for services, such as storage, you will encourage users to look for alternative services and risk ending up with sensitive data stored on lots of flash storage drives or in various places on the cloud. While a little competition may help to reduce costs for an IT department, you have a lot of risk with losing control of technology standards and data privacy. Also, we have no interest in moving dollars around the company just so IT can become a profit center.
>
> That being said, I think it is important to build awareness and transparency of IT costs and encourage a cost-conscious mind-set throughout the company. So instead of charging back for services, we document our expenses for each business unit and share the information with the business unit leaders. It's basically a "paper charge-back" and conveys what the business units would be charged if we elected to charge-back our services. This process has helped us to reduce costs by building awareness and a more cost-conscious user community.

Pharmaceutical vice president Montalto echoes Levine's belief that charge-backs can cause you to lose control of spending. "When you start charging back business units for technology, they see it as an open invitation to demand nonstandard technologies since they are paying for it," she says. "By setting technology standards and centralizing the acquisition and funding, you have better control over what is being purchased."

Despite the challenges with charge-backs, there are many benefits to consider. Charge-backs help an IT department communicate more effectively with its business partners and create a deeper level of transparency. An IT charge-back system forces business leaders to carefully consider what they ask for in terms of products and services. Without a charge-back system, frivolous requests are more difficult to fend off, and you may lose focus on what is really important to the business.

Manage Operational Performance

Just as the president of a division or the COO reviews many operational reports to monitor and manage the business, a CIO needs to consider similar practices to effectively run the shop. Of course, there any many reports a CIO needs to review, so I will focus on the reports that contain critical operational information that should be reviewed on a frequent basis:

- **Help desk tickets.** This report provides a summary of the number of tickets received and resolved by the help desk by application or service area. It should include the number of tickets closed in the past week, closed in the past quarter, and outstanding, along with the aging tickets. The report should include a variance with the aging tickets, relative to your SLA.
- **User satisfaction survey results.** In the next section, I discuss approaches for gathering feedback from end users. Regardless of the approach you choose, you should have reports to review results on a periodic basis. The reports should include a variance to the satisfaction levels from previous surveys.
- **Active projects.** This report should include a list of each project under way with the original and revised targeted completion dates for each major milestone (e.g., scope, analyze, and develop). It should also include actual spending with a variance to the project

budget. Finally, provide a section where project managers can include comments on the progress and project risks.

- **Closed projects.** It is helpful to have a separate report that lists the projects that have been completed in the last 30 days along with the above-mentioned information. This report can help you perform a postmortem on closed projects and apply key findings to future projects. For instance, if your team just finished a project and exceeded its original targeted completion date by 20 days, you can identify the reasons to avoid similar delays in the future or add the time to future projects.

- **System performance.** Have your infrastructure team send you a weekly report on the uptime and response time of each of your critical applications. The report should include a variance to the measurements stated in the SLA.

- **Budget.** In addition to reviewing the project budget just mentioned, you need to routinely compare your department's spending to your overhead budget. It doesn't matter how innovative you are; if you blow your budget time after time, you will most likely lose your job.

Again, a CIO monitors a wide spectrum of operational information, and the previous list represents a small portion of all the information. That being said, if you're not managing your services, projects, and user satisfaction levels on a frequent basis, you're taking a significant risk and will probably be in for a lot of unpleasant surprises.

Develop a Super User Program

I am an ardent believer that your user community should be self-sufficient in the task of training and supporting employees on business application software and related operational processes. While IT is typically responsible for providing training services at the initial rollout of enterprise systems, it is best to equip your end user community with e-learning and instructor-led learning aids to help them be self-sufficient. This practice allows you to keep your IT staffing and travel costs low while ensuring that end users are educated on the software and processes.

I am not suggesting that you don't have a help desk to support end users, but you should try to limit the reasons that users contact the help desk to real technical issues and reduce the number of tickets relating to questions on system use and business process. That is why you have super users.

One of the most common ways to have your users become self-sufficient is to establish a super user program that includes the following components:

- The definition of a super user
- The definition and measurement of program objectives
- A recognition and reward system
- Program maintenance

Let's look at each of the components so you can get a sense of how to put a super user program together for your company.

Help your user community become self-sufficient in the task of training and supporting employees on business application software and related operational processes.

The Definition of a Super User

A super user (SU) is an individual in an organization who is the resident expert for a system or business process. The SU has the following responsibilities:

- Provides the first line of support for users.
- Conducts training for employees on systems and processes.
- Assists local management on system job roles that should be provisioned to new employees by IT.
- Contributes to system user groups and process leadership committees to request and decide on system and process changes.
- Actively participates in performing user acceptance testing (UAT) for new system functionality.
- Helps to communicate the availability of new processes and system features.

A successful SU has the following characteristics:

- Is a strong communicator.
- Advocates continuous improvement.
- Is a high performer.
- Is respected by the local business unit.
- Is patient with others.
- Cares about the success of the company.
- Is detailed oriented.
- Has a proven ability to troubleshoot and resolve technical and process issues.

It is a difficult and demanding role, but it offers great challenge and satisfaction to those who pursue this opportunity. In many cases, SUs will gain job security, recognition, and even promotional opportunities by participating in the program.

The Definition and Measurement of Program Objectives

As with any program, you will need to outline the objectives of an SU program and determine how those objectives will be measured. Having this in writing will help you articulate the reasons for instituting the program, gain sponsorship from local business units, and describe how you will measure the success of the program. Table 5.1 shows some common objectives and measures for an SU program.

A Recognition and Reward System

There are many ways to recognize and reward the contributions of SUs, but failure to recognize and reward SUs will doom the program. Here are a few common methods to shine a light on the SUs:

- A name plate signifying that the employee is a super user.
- A shirt with the SU logo.
- Recognition of SUs at staff meetings and in company newsletters.
- Money (usually in the form of a bonus rather than a raise).

Table 5.1   SU Program Objectives

Objective	Measured By
Provide training services to new and existing employees on business software and related processes.	Level of employee satisfaction with services—surveys and the number of tickets reported to the help desk.
Provide first line of technical support to employees on business software and process-related questions and issues.	Level of employee satisfaction with services—surveys and the number of tickets reported to the help desk.
Assist local management on system job roles that should be provisioned to new employees by IT.	Number of incidents in which an employee does not have an accurate job role assignment.
Contribute to system user groups and process leadership committees to request and decide on system and process changes.	Number of change requests submitted by SU and number approved by governing bodies.
Actively participate in performing UAT for new system functionality.	Number of defects discovered in production that could have been discovered and reported during UAT.
Help to communicate the availability of new process and system features.	Employee awareness of new functionality—employee surveys.

Program Maintenance

One of the challenges companies face with SU programs is that they often fade out shortly after the implementation of an enterprise system. In order to be successful, you need to come up with methods to maintain the program.

Approximately 60 percent of (SAP) shops claim to have an SU program in place. But these programs often fade away or never really work, for a few simple reasons, according to Michael Doane, a longtime SAP consultant who now runs Doane Associates. Doane's firm focuses on helping companies develop SAP centers of excellence, of which a super user program is one component.

"Super users retire, quit, or simply can't hold the role anymore, and no one replaces them," Doane said. "Another reason is the pressure of managers who never really buy in to the system and often tell those employees to get back to their 'real jobs' finally take their toll. The programs fail because of neglect and lack of continuity."[1]

Fluor Corporation has been using SAP software for a decade now. Fluor is well past the go-live "excitement" stage and is now into the maturity model. With the assistance of Doane, Fluor applied these four practices when building its SU program:

1. **Make being a super user "legal."** Fluor decided to "license" its SUs. Employees were nominated and then asked to sign a form (cosigned by their direct supervisor) that authorized them to be SUs and to contribute about 10 to 20 percent of their time to the activity.

2. **Keep it local.** SUs are not superheroes, and they can't be everywhere at once. If there is someone new, like someone transferring into the department, it is extremely valuable to have local people get the new people up to speed.

3. **Line up replacements.** If there is no mechanism to replace someone who quits or transfers, then the SU program will fail through attrition alone. To combat that, every one of Fluor's SUs has nominated a replacement. Also, companies should consider setting a term limit on SUs (e.g., two years) to give employees a break from being SUs and to give others the opportunity to become SUs.

4. **Track the results—before *and* after.** Fluor collected statistics from its help desk: how many times people were calling in, where they were located, and what sorts of questions they were asking. Fluor now uses the data to measure the success of the program. One of Fluor's best practices is that end users aren't allowed to call the help desk directly but must first seek an SU.[2]

I asked pharmaceutical vice president Montalto about her efforts with building an SU program at her company. This is what she said:

We have a community of subject matter experts who help us support our business applications. They provide the first line of support and training services to the end users. We are undergoing a major ERP upgrade this year and plan to leverage our subject matter experts to assist us with the effort. When you think about it, IT doesn't typically use the business application it supports. The actual users of the applications are much better suited to provide front-line support. Of course, we troubleshoot the more complex system issues. Our subject matter experts are highly valued employees and viewed as an extension of our team.

Encourage Feedback

Feedback is a gift. At least, that is what the people giving the constructive criticism tell the people receiving it. For decades, IT has been on the receiving end of feedback through user satisfaction surveys, user group meetings, project reviews, or whatever communication forum companies have cooked up to dish it out to IT professionals. My particular pet peeve is being invited to a meeting with "system issues" on the agenda but no details provided in advance. I always ask for the details—no sense going into a meeting unprepared. I'd like to invite those meeting facilitators to Washington, D.C., to meet with the Internal Revenue Service to discuss their "tax issues" and see how much they like it.

In this section, I will describe two methods for proactively and effectively capturing feedback on IT products and services—and avoiding the unpleasant surprises. One of the methods involves an interactive dialogue so that you can share feedback with your business partners on their use of technology.

Develop and Administer User Surveys

Conducting user satisfaction surveys is a common way to gather feedback from your business partners on technology products and services. You don't need to outsource this task to a professional surveying firm if you are willing to spend a little time and effort on creating and administering the survey. With some planning, you can create an effective survey to gather opinions and ideas from your user organization.

A successful survey produces data that can be translated into valuable information for you and your team. In *How to Conduct Your Own Survey*, Priscilla Salant and Don A. Dillman wrote that you have a better chance of success if you follow these 10 steps:

1. Understand and avoid the four kinds of error.
2. Be specific about what new information you need and why.
3. Choose the survey method that works best for you.
4. Decide whether and how to sample.

5. Write good questions that will provide useful, accurate information.

6. Design and test a questionnaire that is easy and interesting to answer.

7. Put together the necessary resources to carry out your survey in the necessary time frame.

8. Build reports to analyze the data from your questionnaires.

9. Present your results in a way that informs your audience, verbally or in writing.

10. Maintain perspective when putting your plans in place and think through the big picture of what you are attempting to accomplish.[3]

The survey can be conducted on a periodic basis, such as annually. However, certain questions can be asked on a routine basis. For instance, your help desk can routinely send out e-mails to users asking for feedback on the service ticket that was just resolved. Another example is to have your training department send out surveys to class participants asking for feedback on the course and the instructor.

The following is a sample of a user satisfaction survey:

1. Demographics
   - Name, department, title (optional)
   - What division or business unit do you work in?
   - How long have you been at the company?

2. Business application satisfaction
   - On average, how often do you use of each of the following systems? [List systems]
   - Please rate your level of satisfaction in the following areas. The choices for the response are: completely satisfied, satisfied, somewhat dissatisfied, or completely dissatisfied.
     - Ease of use
     - Functionality
     - System response time
     - Reporting
     - Support
     - Business benefits

3. I would recommend this system to another division (yes or no).

There are many publications that provide more detailed material on how to conduct surveys. In addition, certain professional organizations regularly publish the results of studies intended to improve survey methods. These associations and their journals include:

- The American Association for Public Opinion Research and its journal, *Public Opinion Quarterly*.
- The American Statistical Association and its journals, *Journal of the American Statistical Association*, the *American Statistician*, and *Chance*.
- The American Marketing Association and its journal, the *Journal of Marketing Research*.[4]

Your chances of conducting a successful survey improve if you follow the 10 steps listed previously. User satisfaction surveys are an invaluable source of insight for an IT organization. They also demonstrate your interest in listening to your business partners so that you can improve products and services.

For a company to truly exploit technology, it needs to encourage its IT professionals to educate their business partners on what is possible and even provide feedback on how well the company is leveraging existing technology and services. Many CIOs profess that there is no such thing as an IT initiative and that all initiatives are business initiatives. That is a great maxim, but do we truly hold our business partners accountable for using technology to maximize business outcomes?

Retail infrastructure head Levine shares a very interesting process he uses to solicit feedback from end users on IT products and services:

> For years, we have conducted the typical end user surveys and quarterly roundtable discussions with store operators. While we have realized a lot of value from these processes, I wanted my team to have more of a presence in our stores and get a firsthand experience of how employees are using our technologies. So a few years ago we launched our "Adopt-a-Store" program whereby each IT director is responsible for visiting a store on a regular basis. We developed a script for the process, so we can gather specific information from each store visit. The director then shares what they have learned with the rest of the IT leadership team. The Adopt-a-Store program has been an invaluable source of knowledge for us and resulted in many improvements in our technologies and services. It has also helped us to build relationships and trust with our employees who are closest to our customers.

In Chapter 1, I wrote about how CIOs can help their business partners drive business results by identifying and measuring key performance indicators (KPIs). I even suggested that you combine the KPIs into one cohesive and holistic scorecard that allows business leaders to examine their performance with the use of technology and the correlation between the measurements. While the scorecard is a helpful tool to provide feedback to the business user community, I suggest that you go one step further and create an open forum to verbally exchange ideas and feedback with your business partners. In the next section, I describe a program that I refer to as the CIO 360 to help you collaborate with your business partners.

The CIO 360

The CIO 360 process is somewhat similar to the 360 performance review process in which employees receive feedback from the people who work around them. The difference with the CIO 360 process, however, is that it is conducted *in person*, and it is between the IT leaders and the leaders of other business functions that rely on IT products and services. It usually takes the form of a one- or two-day meeting at the business division and has a formal agenda, which is described below.

The CIO 360 process creates an opportunity for business leaders to share feedback on IT products and services, but it is also an opportunity for IT leaders to share feedback on how well the business is leveraging technology to help run the company. Remember, the leaders of other departments are your partners, not your customers, so you should feel comfortable providing your praise and constructive criticism for their performance.

The following is a list of objectives for the CIO 360:

- Gain a better understanding of business performance, business plans, and strategies.
- Build awareness of IT products and services.
- Identify opportunities to further leverage technology to drive business performance.
- Improve awareness of what is working and what is not working. This includes IT's view of how well the business is using IT products and services and complying with policies and processes.

- Share recent IT achievements as well as current plans to address business goals and objectives.
- Foster a strong relationship with business peers.

The CIO 360 does not replace the governance framework described in Chapter 3 but rather complements it by encouraging more communication and engaging with the organization's leaders. While it is natural for participants to identify opportunities for system improvements during this process, you should refrain from usurping the governance bodies that exist for this purpose.

> The CIO 360 process creates an opportunity for business leaders to share feedback on IT products and services, but it is also an opportunity for IT leaders to share feedback on how well the business is leveraging technology to help run the company.

The CIO should work with the business leader to develop an agenda for the meeting. You want to avoid the meeting being perceived as a presentation from IT or, even worse, a gripe session. Here is a sample agenda to consider:

1. Introductions
2. Business overview
   - Business organization chart
   - Financial plan
   - Strategies and objectives
3. IT overview
   - Organization chart
   - Portfolio of products, projects, and services
   - Governance framework
   - Performance measurements (e.g., SLA)
   - IT strategic technology plan and budget
4. Review KPIs
5. Open discussion 1: To what degree is the division maximizing the use of existing technology?
6. Open discussion 2: How can the division further leverage existing technology to address business needs?

7. Open discussion 3: What are some of the challenges the business is facing with the current technology? What are the opportunities for improvement?

8. Open discussion 4: What are some of the concerns that IT has with the business's use or lack of use of existing technology and services?

9. Open discussion 5: What are some new products and services that would help the division achieve its strategic plan? (These ideas need to be processed by the governance committees.)

The CIO 360 is an excellent way to strengthen your relationship with your business partners. It will also make you more aware of the challenges the business is facing and how technology can be a critical enabler of business success.

When you travel to a division to spend time with the leadership team, stay an extra day and have a series of roundtables with the individual contributors and front-line managers in the division. Roundtables were discussed in Chapter 4. To reiterate, roundtables are a great opportunity for you to share information, and they represent an excellent forum for you to *listen* to your audience to gain important feedback. This can help to balance the feedback you receive from the leadership team with the feedback of the people who are consuming your products and services.

Standardize Communications

If I have been successful in writing this book, you will have learned how to strengthen your capabilities to deliver value-added products and services to your business. Two of the capabilities that I share in this regard are how to build a governance framework to help you set priorities with the business and how to establish an SLA to set expectations related to support services.

Despite even the best frameworks and agreements, users will attempt to circumvent the processes to satisfy their interests. For instance, instead of calling the help desk to report issues, they call your team members directly. Another example is that a user interested in changing the design of a system decides to send you an e-mail rather than follow the governance process. In these situations—and others like them—having a set of standard responses that you and your team can send to your users becomes extremely helpful.

A set of standard responses offers the following benefits:

- Creates consistency for your team in its communications with end users.
- Reduces frustration for your team in dealing with users who try to bypass the processes.
- Sets expectations for IT services with users, which ultimately increases satisfaction.
- Maximizes the benefits of IT processes such as governance and support services.
- Increases productivity because less time is spent on responding to inquiries outside the defined processes.

Here is an example of a standard response to a user who has requested support directly from one of your staff members instead of from the help desk:

> Dear Colleague,
>
> It appears that your inquiry should be answered by our help desk team. If you are experiencing a technical issue or have a user-related question, please first report your issue directly to the help desk. Contacting information technology employees directly may cause a delay in resolving your issue. The help desk is in place to make sure your issue is resolved in an expeditious manner.
>
> Our help desk team can provide you with the following assistance:
>
> - Staffing 24 hours a day, 7 days a week with agents trained to respond to your calls, e-mails, chat requests, and online forms.
> - Resolving an average of 75 percent of user issues on the first day.
> - Tracking all requests and communication to ensure that the proper channels are not only aware of your issue but are resolving it as soon as possible.
>
> How to contact the help desk:
>
> - Call the help desk at (add number) 24 hours a day, 7 days a week
> - E-mail the help desk at (add e-mail address)
> - Chat with a help desk agent via help desk live chat

Thank you in advance for taking the time to report your issue directly to the help desk. We look forward to resolving your issue as soon as possible.

Here is a sample list of other standard responses to consider. These templates are available on the companion website:

- Response to a request for system access
- Response to a request for systems training
- Response to a change request from a nongovernance member
- Response to a change request from a governance member
- Confirming receipt of a change request
- Follow-up on an approved change request
- Follow-up on a denied change request

Developing standard responses to user inquiries is straightforward and can be accomplished in a few hours. The trick is to avoid having the responses read like form letters, which may turn off users. That being said, you are influencing their behavior so that you can improve your ability to provide superior services, so some tough love isn't unwarranted.

Build a Shared Service Center

Shared service centers (SSCs) typically involve consolidating and standardized operations, particularly in human resources, accounting, service, and IT. The centers can involve outsourcing relationships or just centralizing services into one function or location. The challenge with many SSCs is that while they do centralize services, they often lack a partnership mind-set, which leaves the users of the services feeling that they are not receiving quality services at a reasonable cost. This section offers some best practices on how to build a high-performance SSC.

Brian R. Lurie, the senior vice president and CIO of Teleflex, gives his view on shared services:

When I joined the company a year ago, we were in many different businesses. Since then we sold off lines of business and have focused solely on the medical device business. We have used the proceeds from the sale of the other businesses to acquire more medical device companies. As part of the transformation, we have created business units for the first time where lines of business, such as vascular access, anesthesia, urology, and respiratory care, are separated so they can focus on the particular customer segment. We also realized, however, that while it made sense to separate sales and marketing, it didn't make sense to separate back-office functions such as IT, HR, and finance. So we created shared services for those common functions, which are leveraged across the business units.

At first, a lot of people were concerned about us not being able to personalize our IT service. That concern turned out to be unnecessary, as our mantra has been all about mass customization and serving the customer. In fact, I used the Ritz-Carlton model for serving the customer. It's not about saving money, but that is certainly a side benefit you get almost without trying—it's about providing the best customer experience. For instance, if I have redundant capabilities all around the world, then I can't get very deep because I have a finite number of people. If I bring them together, then I can have people specialize in areas and become true experts, thereby providing an even greater level of service for my customers when they need it.

While IT is usually organized as an SSC, it isn't always the case and greatly depends on the organizational structure of the company. IT organizational structures are discussed in Chapter 2, and best practices for IT have been interspersed throughout the book to help you build an effective IT SSC. Regardless of whether IT is organized as an SSC, it can be a key enabler to the business for forming an SSC of its own to serve multiple processes, such as human resources, accounting, and service.

Expect Resistance

You may find that while leaders are happy to consolidate services into their regions, they are not supportive when it comes to centralizing services at headquarters. They fear the loss of control will lead to operational issues and affect business results. I worked with a president who had done a stellar job consolidating functions into his region, resulting in head-count reductions, better deals with vendors, and other cost savings. When the company decided to replicate the strategy by centralizing the very same functions to headquarters, the regional president was not very supportive. He was experiencing the same feelings his divisions experienced when he decided to regionalize the functions. While change is never easy, it can be softened by setting clear expectations of service levels.

Establish SLAs

Formalize the supplier–buyer relationship by collaboratively developing SLAs (as discussed earlier in this chapter) that document service expectations and responsibilities.

Establish and Continually Measure KPIs

The KPIs will ensure that the service delivered consistently meets or exceeds internal shared service and user expectations. Using bidirectional KPIs will help in performing root cause analyses, developing action plans, and enhancing the shared accountability for shared service performance. The KPI program described in Chapter 1 will help you define this part of the program.

Teleflex CIO Lurie bets his bonus on customer satisfaction. "We have a dashboard that we monitor on a routine basis, including KPIs such as how long customers were on hold, system uptime, and customer satisfaction ratings," he says. "Our bonuses are based on how well our customers believe we have done our job. We survey our customers on each of our actions, including service tickets and project activities."

Conclusion

Taking the steps to transition from a centralized business model to a user-focused, measurement-driven SSC with shared accountability for end-to-end process performance can yield significant benefits. The practices described here build on the centralization and standardization activities that will have been completed to create a centralized business model in the first place. The steps outlined in this chapter take the centralization and standardization levers a step further, combining them with other valuable tools to ensure that the proper measurements are in place and are visible and transparent.

By using the techniques and tools described, organizations can create a new, partner-centered culture within shared services. Furthermore, developing the ongoing dialogue and supplier-partner relationship between the SSC and its users will make all of the benefits of using the shared services model to drive high performance both attainable and sustainable.

Top Plays

- SLAs help IT articulate the levels of services it delivers and how services will be measured and communicated.
- A super user program can help you lower IT costs and increase satisfaction throughout your company.
- User satisfaction surveys can be an instrumental way to collect feedback from your user community.
- Make the feedback process with leaders interactive by conducting the CIO 360.
- An IT charge-back is a financial management strategy to describe how costs are incurred and recovered by IT in support of the business.
- Creating standard responses to user inquiries can help you set expectations and achieve consistency in your communication with end users.
- An SSC with a user-focused, measurement-driven approach will help you yield significant benefits over a centralized approach.

Notes

1. Courtney Bjorlin, "How to Build an SAP Super User Program That Will Last," *Americas' Super User Program (ASUG) News,* July 1, 2011.
2. *Ibid.*
3. Priscilla Salant and Don A. Dillman, *How to Conduct Your Own Survey* (New York: John Wiley & Sons, 1994), 11.
4. *Ibid.*

Chapter 6

Step 6: Protect

Risk is like fire: If controlled it will help you; if uncontrolled it will rise up and destroy you.

—*Theodore Roosevelt*

Protect: Manage and minimize risks so that your company can continue to operate effectively and protect its reputation.

Risk surrounds every business every day—from network attacks and viruses to data loss. An important part of IT's job is to manage and minimize these risks so that the company can continue to operate effectively and protect its reputation. This chapter describes the risks that an IT department must manage to protect its company's interests and some strategies to ensure minimal effect on the business in the event of an IT service interruption. It also explains the methods for addressing the mounting risks with fast-moving trends, including cloud computing, social media, and mobility.

The National Institute of Standards and Technology (NIST) developed a risk management guide for IT systems. An effective risk management process is an important component of a successful IT security program. The principal goal of an organization's risk management process should be to protect the organization and its ability to perform its mission, not just to protect its IT assets.

Therefore, the risk management process should not be treated primarily as a technical function carried out by the IT experts who operate and manage the IT system, but as an essential management function of the organization. NIST has defined risk management as follows:

> Risk management is the process that allows IT managers to balance the operational and economic costs of protective measures and achieve gains in mission capability by protecting the IT systems and data that support their organizations' mission.[1]

Define Risk Management Goals

According to control objectives for information and related technology, the following IT goals should be instituted to manage IT-related business risk:

- Account for and protect all IT assets.
- Protect the achievement of IT objectives.
- Establish clearly the effect on the business of risks to IT objectives and resources.
- Ensure that critical and confidential information is withheld from those who should not have access to it.
- Ensure that automated business transactions and information exchanges can be trusted.
- Ensure that IT services and infrastructure can properly resist and recover from failures that result from error, deliberate attack, or disaster.
- Ensure minimum effect on the business in the event of an IT service disruption or change.

The goals should be considered by every IT department to help minimize and respond to risks.

Be Transparent with Risk Management

In risk management, a threat is merely the potential for the exercise of a particular vulnerability. Threats in themselves are not actions; they must be coupled with threat sources to become dangerous. This is an important distinction when assessing and managing risks, since each threat source may be associated with a different likelihood, which, as will be demonstrated, affects risk assessment and risk management.

Just as you measure and report on the service level agreement (SLA) benchmarks discussed in Chapter 5, you should track and share performance with managing risks. The complexity of your risk management program will depend on whether your company is publicly traded as well as the type of industry it is in. For instance, while a publicly traded company needs to adhere to Sarbanes-Oxley requirements, a publicly traded U.S. pharmaceutical company is also required to be in compliance with Food and Drug Administration regulations.

It is important that risk management is fully incorporated in your IT management practices and not something that is looked at only when your department is being audited by internal or external auditors. The best IT shops are proactive with risk management and work with their auditors to identify controls to measure. An example of a control may be to ensure the segregation of duties with system user profiles. Here are some benchmarks to consider:

- Number of IT controls to measure.
- Number and percentage of passed controls from prior audit.
- Prior audit opinion (e.g., satisfactory or unsatisfactory).
- Number of failed controls with approved action plans developed. Catalog each failed control by severity.
- Number of repeat audit findings.

The best IT shops are proactive with risk management and work with their auditors to identify controls to measure.

Once you have identified the benchmarks to be measured, monitor them carefully and report on the results using your communication program. Be sure to share both the good and the bad news to maintain credibility and trust with employees throughout the organization.

Monitor Risk Mitigation Activities

Auditors have a maxim: "Trust but verify." When it comes to action plans for failed controls, CIOs have a responsibility to proactively monitor progress with the action plans. Most plans are written with targeted completion dates, so having recurring checkpoint meetings based on the target dates will help you keep a pulse on the activity. Meetings drive deliverables; they establish deadlines, so use meetings to verify that staff members are taking risk management seriously.

Megatrends and the Risks

Nearly two years ago, Maryfran Johnson, the editor of *CIO* magazine, coined the term "mega-trend trio" to describe mobility, cloud computing, and social media.[2] Today the megatrend trio is certainly absorbing the minds of CIOs around the globe. Keeping sensitive data safe and protecting a company's reputation has become increasingly challenging as enterprises increase their use of these technologies. For this reason, the remaining portion of this chapter is devoted to identifying and managing the risks associated with cloud computing, mobility, and social media.

Safeguard Cloud Computing

Cloud computing represents the next major change that will enable IT to continue to enable business innovation and competitive advantage while reducing overall costs. CIOs need to leverage this new computing paradigm from both a tactical and a strategic perspective.

There has been a tremendous amount of research conducted on cloud computing, and it has certainly earned a great deal of hype over the last few years. In "Top Threats to Cloud Computing 1.0," Cloud Security Alliance, identified seven top security-related threats for cloud computing:

1. **Insecure application programming interfaces.** Criminals continue to leverage new technologies to improve their reach, avoid detection, and improve the effectiveness of their activities.
2. **Insecure interfaces and application programming interfaces (APIs).** While most providers strive to ensure that security

is well integrated in their service models, it is critical for consumers of those services to understand the security implications associated with the usage, management, orchestration, and monitoring of cloud services.

3. **Malicious insiders.** The effect that malicious insiders can have on an organization is considerable, given their level of access and ability to infiltrate the organization and its assets.

4. **Shared technology vulnerabilities.** Disk partitions, central processing unit (CPU) caches, graphics processing units (GPUs), and other shared elements were never designed for strong compartmentalization. As a result, attackers focus on how to affect the operations of other cloud customers and gain unauthorized access to data.

5. **Data loss or leakage.** Data loss or leakage can have a devastating effect on a business. Beyond the damage it can cause to one's brand and reputation, a loss could significantly affect employee, partner, and customer morale and trust.

6. **Service and traffic hijacking.** Account and service hijacking, usually with stolen credentials, remains a top threat. With stolen credentials, attackers can often access critical areas of deployed cloud computing services, allowing them to compromise the confidentiality, integrity, and availability of those services.

7. **Unknown risk profile.** When a cloud service is adopted, the features and functionality may be well advertised, but what about the details or compliance of the internal security procedures, configuration hardening, patching, auditing, and logging? Security by obscurity may be low effort, but it can result in unknown exposures. It may also impair the in-depth analysis required by highly controlled or regulated operational areas.[3]

I recently met with Michael Gabriel, the CIO of Home Box Office, the nation's most successful premium television company. Home Box Office delivers two 24-hour pay television services—HBO and Cinemax. HBO continues to take advantage of the latest technological innovations with advances that include the availability of HBO programming online though HBO GOSM (Gtk OpenStreetMap) and MAX GOSM, as well as HBO on Demand and Cinemax on Demand in high definition.

Gabriel explains how he manages the risks associates with cloud computing:

> Since you are outsourcing a function, you potentially have less control over it in terms being able to dedicate resources and respond to it outside the defined service level agreement [SLA]. So managing the risks of cloud computing means you need to have a very good understanding of what service level agreements you need to have in place, in terms of operational support and responsiveness. We outsourced a very dynamic part of our business because we were concerned that we may not be in the position to scale our internal architecture to meet our growing needs. The benefit of the scalability and responsiveness of an organization that has infrastructure available in multiple locations with high levels of redundancy and failover outweighs the potential risks of cloud computing.
>
> I also believe a very well-thought-out SLA is essential to helping you manage risks with cloud computing. The SLA must cover, in addition to performance criteria, data security, disaster recovery, portability, and responsiveness. The absence of a comprehensive SLA increases your risks with both cost and service delivery.

David Colville, the CIO of Nestlé Waters North America (NWNA), says that "the biggest risk with cloud computing is security and privacy. It is particularly challenging when hosting outside the United States, where the agreements are governed by the laws and regulations of another country. Fortunately for us, most technology offerings are hosted in the United States, either on our private cloud or by third-party hosting providers."

He believes in balancing SLAs with positive and negative reinforcements:

> I would much rather be in a position where I am paying providers an incentive for overachieving on services than collecting punitive dollars for underperforming. Once a provider underperforms, you have already disappointed your business partners, and a few thousand dollars isn't going to help you or your business. If you incorporate too many penalties into an agreement with a provider, they are just going to build it into their price or safeguards in terms of their SLA.

Colville believes in establishing agreements with providers that allow for shared risk while encouraging high performance and value through incentives.

| International Data Corporation predicted that the cloud security market will grow to $4.8 billion in 2014.

The cloud security market will continue to grow as companies recruit the help of technology partners to address specific cloud issues, such as securing access or negotiating SLAs. In a recent study, International Data Corporation predicted that the cloud security market will grow to $4.8 billion in 2014. So if you aren't already using cloud security services, you will most likely be in the market for it in the next few years. Selecting the right partners is a crucial step as you plan, migrate, and operate safely and successfully in the era of cloud computing.

Safeguard Mobility

Mobility is one of the hottest trends, and it is truly a paradigm shift in data access services. It's also one of the most challenging topics for CIOs to deal with in effectively managing security concerns. According to Gartner Group, some 5 billion smartphones were in use in 2010, and 6.7 billion are projected to be in use by 2015.

According to the Cellular Telecommunications and Internet Association's semiannual survey, as of June 2011 there were more wireless subscriber connections (327.6 million) than people in the United States and its territories (315.5 million). Wireless data traffic grew 111 percent, and the number of smartphones and wireless-enabled handheld devices grew 57 percent. Both serve as more evidence for why the U.S. wireless industry needs to purchase more spectrum from the U.S. government: so we can meet the nation's demand while also helping the economy.

The growth is based on the increase in demand from workers wanting to work on smartphones instead of being tethered to a desktop computer or having to lug around a laptop computer. The growth in demand for mobile computing devices and applications is only fueling the concerns of the IT leaders who are responsible for protecting company data.

NWNA's Colville says the following:

The exploitation of mobile devices and the lack of tools and standards for mobile data management continues to be a major challenge for IT departments. Aside from being able to remotely wipe devices if they are lost or stolen, we are left with mitigating the risks through policy rather than technology in many cases. However, you are much better off allowing your users to securely access company data through their mobile devices rather than to prevent the use of mobile technology. If you try to prevent mobilization, users will find a way to download confidential data to their devices, and you won't have any way to wipe the device if they are lost or stolen or if the employee leaves the company. That would be a bigger problem.

Although it is clear that an IT leader takes on risks in allowing mobile access to sensitive data, there is much greater risk in prohibiting such access. HBO's Gabriel agrees:

Not unlike cloud computing, you need to look at the opportunity the technology presents in relation to the risks. Failing to recognize the trend of practically everyone using mobile devices in their personal lives is a big risk for CIOs—it would demonstrate that the CIO is out of touch with the way the world is operating. That being said, having business information made available on mobile devices, with each device having a different level of security protection, both in terms of transmission and storage of the information, presents tremendous risk. To mitigate these risks we are partnering with human resources, legal, and finance to make sure we understand the challenges with mobile computing and costs of protecting company information. The benefits of mobile computing for your company have to outweigh the risks of making it available.

Richard Lattmann, the associate vice president of U.S. infrastructure services at Sanofi, offers a similar perspective on the risks of mobile computing:

Mobility is a major focus for most companies. I think the biggest challenge for IT leaders is to avoid getting in the way of productive uses of mobile computing. It's spreading like wildfire, and I don't think any company can contain it—nor should they. Companies don't have to own the devices; they just need to own the access point to the network. I anticipate the next generation workstations will not involve replacing all our equipment; it will be a partial refresh—meaning, some users will bring their own devices, others will have their company-owned laptops replaced with tablets, and desktop users may receive very thin client devices.

Panda Security, the cloud security company, has released a report in participation with other members of Spain's Cyber-National Advisory

Council on the history, current state, and future of mobile malware. Now available for the first time in the United States, the report on smartphone malware aims to raise awareness of the threats affecting mobile devices and provides tips individuals can follow to avoid falling victim to mobile threats.[4]

To protect your mobile device, the report offers a list of best practices:

- Enable access protection measures such as a PIN or a password (if possible).
- Configure the smartphone to automatically lock after a minute or so of being idle.
- Before installing or using new smartphone apps or services, check their reputation. Install applications only from trusted sources.
- Pay attention to the security permissions requested by every application and service you install.
- Keep your operating system and software applications up-to-date.
- Disable features not in use, such as Bluetooth, infrared, or Wi-Fi.
- If you have Bluetooth enabled, set your device to be hidden and password-protect it.
- Make regular backup copies of your important files.
- Encrypt sensitive information whenever possible.
- Use call and short message service (SMS) encryption software.
- Whenever possible, do not store sensitive information on the smartphone. Make sure it is not cached locally.
- Erase all information from the smartphone before you get rid of it.
- In the event that your phone is lost or stolen, inform your service provider and give it your device's international mobile equipment identity (IMEI) number to block it.
- Use remote or automatic deletion of data (after several failed log-in attempts).
- Monitor the smartphone for anomaly detection.
- Check your account activity frequently to detect fraud.
- Be aware of the risks associated with these devices and use them correctly.
- Take all necessary precautions when opening e-mail messages, opening SMS attachments, or clicking links. (Remember that this was one of the entry points of the Zeus-Mitmo virus.)

- Be wary of any files, links, or numbers received from unsolicited e-mail or SMS messages.
- Avoid using untrusted Wi-Fi networks.
- Take smartphones into account when establishing your corporate security policy.

Smartphones are much more than just phones and should be treated more like computers, given the applications and confidential data that reside on them.

Safeguard Social Media

The new reality of business is that the bottom line is driven by what we know about our customers and how well-connected we are to them. The reach and power of social media channels is extraordinary. Facebook has more than 800 million active users, with more than 50 percent of the users logging on every day. Twitter has over 200 million registered users. LinkedIn reaches over 120 million users, and more than half of LinkedIn members are currently located outside the United States. These channels provide tremendous opportunity for companies to promote their products, interact with customers, and build brand loyalty. With this opportunity, however, comes increased risk.

The social media are no longer a new platform, and the pioneers have certainly taken the arrows for the rest of us. There are many lessons to learn from the trailblazers. Perhaps the sagest advice is to develop a multilayered approach that maximizes social media's benefits while protecting your company's reputation. At minimum, you need to institutionalize a social media risk management program that combines technical solutions, policies, and resources.

Social media's greatest risk is to a company's reputation. Disgruntled employees, fraudsters, crooked competitors, and even human error are often to blame. The consequences can be far-reaching: loss of sales, damage to your reputation, loss of confidence in your products, and much more. According to a *Social Media Today* article, a social media risk management program should include the following five components:

1. **Social media monitoring.** Continual monitoring of social media sites, blogs, forums, news feeds, and other sites for instances where your company or brand is mentioned, including pictures and videos.

2. **Domain name monitoring.** Continual monitoring of global domain name registration databases to identify all newly registered domains that could threaten your brand and intellectual property.
3. **Traffic insight.** Tools that help you collect data on who is visiting your website and where they came from.
4. **Threat management portal.** Secure, centralized online management tools to help identify, track, and manage incidents and coordinate responses.
5. **Emergency response team.** Internal or external experts to help you prevent and eliminate online issues that threaten your company.[5]

NWNA's Colville says the following about the social media practices at his company:

We are entering an era when people would rather visit your Facebook page than your website. You have to find a way to engage with your customers on a personal level while protecting your reputation. It's part of the ante of today's economy. Most companies will approach social networking from multiple facets, including brand promotion, recruiting, and crisis management. In global companies, the practice of social networking becomes even more complex as individual geographies want to use the technology for their purposes. While social networking should not be seen as an IT initiative, we need to help the business collaborate and strategize so we are using the technology responsibility and securely and we also don't wind up with a thousand Facebook pages.

Social media present unique challenges for business and IT leaders. Having a well-thought-out social media strategy and risk management program will better equip you in addressing the threats of this channel while reaping its many benefits.

Top Plays

• Risk management must be fully incorporated into your IT management practices and not considered something that is looked at only when your department is being audited by internal or external auditors.

(continued)

- Once you have identified the risks to be measured, monitor them carefully and report on the results using your communication program.
- Cloud computing represents the next major change that will enable IT to continue to enable business innovation and competitive advantage while reducing overall costs.
- Selecting the right partners is a crucial step as you plan, migrate, and operate safely and successfully in the era of cloud computing.
- The risk of prohibiting access to company data via mobile devices is greater than the inherent risks of mobile computing.
- Develop a multilayered approach that maximizes social media's benefits while protecting your company's reputation.

Notes

1. Gary Stoneburner, Alice Goguen, and Alexis Feringa, *Risk Management Guide for Information Technology Systems* (Gaithersburg, MD: National Institute of Standards and Technology, 2002), 4.

2. Maryfran Johnson, "CIOs Respond to 'Mega-Trend Trio'": Mobile, Cloud and Social," *CIO*, August 27, 2010.

3. Cloud Security Alliance, "Top Threats to Cloud Computing 1.0," white paper, March 2010, https://cloudsecurityalliance.org/topthreats/csathreats.v1.0.pdf.

4. "Seven Tips on Keeping Your Mobile Devices Secure: Report on Smartphone Malware," *TechJournal*, June 9, 2011.

5. Greg Barrow, "5 Benefits of a Social Media Risk Management Program," *Social Media Today*, February 17, 2011, http://socialmediatoday.com/gregbarrow/271023/5-benefits-social-media-riskmanagement-program.

Chapter 7

Step 7: Grow

My main job was developing talent. I was a gardener providing water and other nourishment to our top 750 people. Of course, I had to pull out some weeds, too.

—*Jack Welch*

Grow: Attract, motivate, and retain a talented IT team that works toward a common vision and mission.

During my career in IT, I have developed a passion for building high-performance teams, and it has always been my top priority. With it, everything is possible. Without it you can count on failing at the other best practices described in this book. A sound talent management program starts with establishing a clear vision for your department and engaging employees by defining how they fit into this vision.

This chapter describes four practical strategies for talent management: standardizing job descriptions, developing a role-based training program, rotating your staff, and retaining critical skills. It's been a successful blueprint for me because it builds on the other six steps described in this book and brings together the methods, processes, and activities required to build a high-performance team—the ultimate competitive advantage.

Standardize Job Descriptions

Chapter 1 described an approach to defining the vision, mission, and goals of an IT department. With the purpose of your department defined, you can go about identifying the types of human resources you will need to achieve your vision. Job descriptions serve as the basis for all other talent acquisition and development strategies that an organization can create.

When Greg Fell joined Terex Corporation as its first CIO six years ago, he was tasked with establishing a unified IT organization where employees work toward a common vision. At the time, Terex operated as a holding company, with each of the sixty business sites having its own IT department. "Each business had a lot of autonomy when it came to IT, which resulted, not surprisingly, in a lack of technology architecture, and standards, including things as fundamental as a company-wide computer network or e-mail system," says Greg.

Greg knew he would have to spend his first few years at Terex implementing the technology and services that most CIOs take for granted when joining a new company. He also knew he needed to build his team at corporate headquarters very quickly and establish a partnership with the IT departments at the business sites. He adds:

> I created an IT career development framework to attract, motivate, and retain staff. The framework consists of both a managerial and technical [function] and clarifies the responsibilities and qualifications of each position. It's been an invaluable tool in helping me recruit new employees and motivate existing employees by giving them a clear development path at corporate and at the business sites. I also developed an IT leadership development program, which I personally taught along with others, to help my staff strengthen their critical skills such as people management, recruiting, and negotiation.

Standardizing jobs within each function (e.g., development and infrastructure) will make it easier for you to design programs such as training, performance management, and compensation assessments.

I asked Michael Gabriel, the CIO of HBO, about the talent man-agement strategies at HBO, including identifying core skills for each job. Here is what he shared with me:

> We have a very formal talent management program in place where every job has a list of key skills and competencies that contribute to performance of the job. Every staff member is assessed on how well they are performing with respect to those skills and competencies. Development maps are created by supervisors in conjunction with our head of IT professional development and monitored throughout an individual's career. The assessments and develop-ment maps are also used utilized as a basis to help supervisors determine if an individual has a sufficient level of expertise to be promoted to the next level.
>
> While we are continuing to develop everyone in the department, I am focusing more of my attention on developing employees in the three jobs that I believe contribute to the success of a project: the project manager, the business analyst, and the technical architect. I refer to these jobs as the "triangle of project success." A project will have a greater chance of success if the individuals in each of these jobs perform well.
>
> When developing a talent management program, I suggest you focus on fewer jobs and skills initially rather than attempting to create a comprehensive program. By focusing your attention on fewer areas, you will be able to make demonstrable improvements in critical skills and then scale the program to address other areas.

Standardizing jobs within each function will make it easier for you to design programs such as training, performance management, and compensation assessments.

For the purposes of this chapter, let's define a *job* as generic, in the sense that many employees can hold the same type of job. However, the term *position* is considered to be unique; only one person can hold a specific position in the company. The following is a list of sections for a job description:

- **Soft skills.** Many soft skills are shared across the functions, so add these requirements in each job description. Software skills are the emotional quotient (EQ) aspects of a job, such as listening skills or dealing with ambiguity. The more senior the role, the more pro-gressive the language of the requirements should be. Of course, roles may differ in terms of some of the EQ requirements. As an example, a developer may not be required to have presentation skills, whereas these skills are critical for a business systems analyst.

- **Functional skills.** After you have standardized the soft skills, determine which functional skills are required for each job role with each function. These functional skills are typically specific to each area, but there is usually some overlap. Just be sure everyone within a function shares the same basic job requirements. For instance, a business systems analyst in the IT sales area should have the basic requirements as, for instance, a business systems analyst in the IT purchasing area. Some of the requirements may be relationship management, requirement gathering, testing, and project management.

- **Save the technical requirements for the position descriptions.** Standardized job descriptions should be technically agnostic. That is, the descriptions should be free of any reference to specific technologies, such as SAP, Citrix, or Java. Remember, these are job descriptions, not position descriptions. Position descriptions are much more specific. As such, you may want to create a separate document or an appendix clearly describing each position in your department (e.g., Citrix administrator). Position descriptions are often used in the postings for the positions when recruiting for a position, so it's important that the particular technical requirements are documented.

- **Qualifications and other elements.** Of course, you will need to consider the references for experience and education. Job descriptions also contain information on working conditions, travel requirements, and other elements that are important to your organization.

- **Side-by-side comparisons.** Employees like to understand not only what is required of them in their current role but also what is expected of them in the next rung on the proverbial career ladder. For that reason, a good practice is to build a job matrix that clearly lays out each job across the page and the requirements (e.g., soft skills and functional skills) down the page.

Once you spell out the requirements for each job in the matrix, the employees will clearly understand the available career paths in the department and what skills are necessary to be considered for a promotion. However, remind the employees that the primary intention of the job matrix is to help them clearly understand what is needed to maximize their contributions in their *current* role.

Develop a Role-Based Training Program

As companies continue to scrutinize their budgets, funding for IT training is usually the first thing to go and the last thing to come back. Don't make this mistake. In this case, I am speaking of education services for your IT staff, not the end-user community. The paradox is that training is usually a top priority for many of your staff members.

So how can you build a training program for your staff that is effective, appreciated, and economical? Earlier, I mentioned that job descriptions serve as the basis for many talent management programs, including training. This section will describe the best practices for developing and implementing a cost-effective and comprehensive training program for your staff.

Building a Training Program

Simply put, you need to identify a training component for each skill requirement mentioned in the job descriptions. A litany of research has been conducted on learning methods, so I will summarize by pointing out that training is generally delivered in the form of six methods—books, videos, classroom-based instructor-led training (ILT) courses, e-learning, webinars, and experience—or a hybrid of any of these forms. The learning methods can be a mix of internally and externally developed material. I am sure there are variations of these methods, but let's keep it simple for the purposes of this book and to get you started with your program.

The least expensive and most sustainable delivery method is e-learning. A 2011 survey by the Human Capital Media Advisory Group, the research arm of *Chief Learning Officer* magazine, showed that while nearly half of the respondents chose classroom-based ILT as their company's primary learning delivery method from 2009 to 2010, the overall trend has been downward. The respondents cited increased expenses and a drop in effectiveness as the reason for the decline.[1]

While critics will argue that participants will retain more information using one method or the other, most will agree that a good training program should include a variety of methods to satisfy the different learning styles of the participants. For this reason, I will use the term *learning tool* to be representative of the variety of methods.

Training is the top priority for many of your staff members, or at least one of the top priorities.

Common Learning Tools: Soft Skills

The first step in building a training program is to analyze the job descriptions in each of the technology functions, such as infrastructure, development, and business analysis and identify the learning tools that satisfy the common soft-skill requirements. Typically, these soft skills can be applied to a variety of functional roles and are also the basis of the performance review process. Using a common set of competencies—for example, being customer driven, managing conflict, listening, and having an action orientation—can be applied to a variety of roles.

Keep in mind that a department will have different expectations for a level-one infrastructure engineer than for the director of the function. For example, you will most likely want an infrastructure engineer to be action oriented on tasks, whereas a director will be required to be action oriented with people and projects. Please note that a comprehensive training program includes a role-based curriculum for all levels, including your leadership team. As such, you will need to find successive learning tools for each skill (e.g., beginner, intermediate, and advanced action-orientation-skill e-learning courses).

Common Learning Tools: Technical Skills

After identifying the competencies and tools for the common soft skills, look to identify courses for common technical skills (e.g., IT infrastructure library, control objectives for information and related technology, Program Management Institute [PMI], testing, and compliance) that are necessary for all of the various technology functions. These are not soft

skills, but rather job-specific skills that are common throughout a particular IT function (like infrastructure) or even the entire IT department.

Function-Specific Learning Tools. Function-specific skills are
where learning paths start to deviate from the other common skills.
They are typically specific to each function (e.g., infrastructure or
development), but there can be some overlap. What is important is that
everyone in a function (e.g., business analysis) shares the same basic job
requirements. For instance, a business systems analyst in the IT sales
area should have the same basic requirements as a similar role in the IT
purchasing area (e.g., relationship management, requirement gathering,
testing, or project management). If the standardized job descriptions are
well written, the task of identifying the learning tools will be easier.

Avoid the Pitfall of Overdoing the Curriculum. A common
pitfall with curriculum development is attempting to identify common
learning methods for every technology used in your department. This
amount of customization is not necessary when only a few employees
use the technology. Time is better spent on identifying the courses that
are needed by most of the people in your department.

Recognition and Reward Learning

Finally, identify methods of reward or recognition to build excitement
for the training program. Consider establishing a system whereby the
employees achieve a membership level (e.g., bronze, silver, or gold) after
successfully completing a set number of courses. With such a system
in place, you can host periodic luncheons to celebrate membership
achievement. Once the employees learn that their peers are being
recognized for investing in their careers, they will be inspired take a
course or two themselves.

Mandatory or Not?

Companies have different policies and practices for training, but in my
experience, most do not make training mandatory except for those

who are required by law, for system access, or for education on company policies. Aside from these instances, it's best to leave learning opportunities as optional but highly encouraged and supported by your management team. People need to take responsibility for their own careers. You know the old adage: "You can lead a horse to water, but you can't make him drink."

Staying Current

Whether by the formal training just described or by a self-learning type of program, you need to stay abreast of both the IT industry and the industry that your company is in. Staying current with one but not the other is not good enough—you have to stay current in both areas.

Consumers of technology (read: your business partners) are becoming more and more tech savvy. They have the latest gadgets, and their news feeds are incorporating the latest information in the world of technology. You can't pick up a copy of the *Wall Street Journal* or *BusinessWeek* without seeing an advertisement for technology. Your business partners have seen the words *virtualization* and *cloud computing* hundreds of times—even before they had a clue about what the terms meant.

I realize the incredibly fast pace of technology makes it very difficult to stay current with the latest news, events, and trends. However, there are ways to keep up-to-date without experiencing information overload. Here are some tips:

- **Subscribe to an industry research service.** The easiest way to stay informed with technology and business is to subscribe to a research service such as Gartner and Forrester. These services are not inexpensive, so this opportunity will depend on your budget.
- **Subscribe to industry magazines.** Again, I am referring to both technology and business news. Most of the industry magazines are free as long as you qualify to receive them, which is typically based on your title and the size of your company. Even if you don't qualify for a hard-copy version of the magazine, the publisher typically offers an online version without requiring a subscription. In fact, many publishers are going strictly digital.

- **Subscribe to news feeds.** The quickest and easiest way to get the latest news and events is to setup RSS feeds that are customized to your interests. They don't cost a dime, and they give you a stock-ticker experience, with the news flashing by on your screen. I must admit that I am bit of a news junkie, so this is my preferred method.

- **Subscribe to blogs.** Blogs provide another great source of industry information. I subscribe to dozens of blogs that send me alerts when someone creates a new post. It can get a bit overwhelming at times, so I tend to fine-tune the alerts to specific areas of interest.

- **Ask your kids.** No, I am not joking. Think about it: Your kids probably know more about the latest consumer technologies than you do. They learn about it by spending so much time on social media sites such as Facebook, Twitter, and YouTube. My son was showing me a video clip of a reporter's prediction of the latest iPad on a social media site well before it hit the mainstream media news feeds.

- **Don't read paperbacks on an airplane.** You get a lot of uninterrupted time on an airplane to catch up on the news. Don't waste it by reading a novel. Bring lots of industry-related magazines and books with you—either hard copies or saved on your mobile device. You will be surprised how much productive reading you can get done in a two- or three-hour flight.

- **Read in your spare time.** Okay, I realize you need some downtime, and you deserve it, but just like when you were in school, you need to do your homework. I am not suggesting you bring work home. In fact, I believe *you should never bring work home.* What I am saying is that when you are sitting on your patio or in your den, pick up and read an article in an industry magazine a few days a week. In fact, I bring home all of my industry magazines, and that's where I read them. I don't know about you, but I can't think of the last time I was able to sit in my office and actually read an industry magazine. I get way too antsy thinking about all of the work I need to do. So I stick the magazines in my briefcase and bring them home. They usually find their way into the "home office" that has a sink, if you get my meaning.

The More You Teach, the More You Learn

- **Go to industry conferences.** As mentioned earlier, some people learn by reading, while others learn by listening to others. I happen to be a reader, but I do enjoy attending a good conference here and there to pick up the latest information. It's also a great way to network with your peers. I have found that I tend to learn more over a meal with a few acquaintances than during a keynote address. Keep your eyes out for free regional conferences.
- **Teach to learn.** I know, it sounds like an oxymoron. When I am asked to lecture at a conference, I tend to get nervous and find myself researching the topic so that I sound semi-intelligent when giving the talk. For some odd reason, I keep getting invited to speak on cloud computing. When I started speaking on the topic, I knew the basics about the different types of clouds and deployment models—and could even describe my personal experiences with cloud computing over the last few years. However, after researching the topic for my talks, I became more and more entrenched in the topic of cloud technologies and found myself citing the latest advances, the risks, the pitfalls, and the opportunities. I could even rattle off examples of how businesses capitalized on this new paradigm shift in computing to enter new markets and become more competitive. The point is, the more you teach, the more you learn. So the next time you are invited to speak at a conference, go for it—even if you aren't an expert on the topic.

Rotate Your Staff

As the economy slowly shows signs of improvement, your IT staff members will inevitably question whether they should explore new opportunities. The management challenge that we face is that IT professionals possess skills that are relatively transferable from one industry to another, so if you're in a hard-hit industry, you have more risk of not retaining your top talent as other industries improve faster. So how do you retain your IT staff in today's unpredictable economy?

Build a Job Rotation Program

Job rotation programs are designed to move employees from job to job within a company as a vehicle to attract, retain, and motivate staff. Rotation programs give employees an opportunity to explore other careers, avoid job boredom, develop competencies, foster their career growth, and improve their talents in an organization. A well-designed job rotation program can have a profound impact on job satisfaction, productivity, and retention. Rotations are different from normal job openings because here the job opening is created by two employees expressing a desire to move into each other's jobs.

Where Do I Start? First, assemble a small, cross-functional team of individual contributors and managers to define the program. The team can help you study the topic, define specific objectives, establish the process, and make sure that whatever you eventually put in place will be an effective program.

> Rotation programs give employees an opportunity to explore other careers, avoid job boredom, develop competencies, foster their career growth, and improve their talents in an organization.

Defining the Objectives. While the name of the program clearly implies its intention, it does not convey why such a program is necessary for your company. It is important that you clearly emphasize this. Organizations put rotation programs in place to attain different objectives. The team that you assemble to build the program can help you identify and communicate the objectives. Merely saying that the program will be designed to help retain employees is not sufficient, because no one will understand how such a program will help retain employees. Besides, retaining employees is a goal or an outcome, not an objective.

An example of an objective of a job rotation program is to broaden an individual's knowledge of other functions in the IT department, which in turn will help him or her to become more valuable to the organization. And in the current economic climate, where people are concerned about job security, increasing their worth to an organization is important.

Establishing a Process. After you have sufficiently studied rotation programs and are ready to design your own, carefully consider the type of process that you will need. Some companies have very informal rotation programs. In these companies, the culture itself encourages employees to move from one job to another. There may be enough natural movement that a highly structured program is not necessary—*too* much structure may even be viewed as an impediment in this type of culture. However, it is arguable that some amount of structure is necessary in any type of culture so that the employees understand *how* to make a move into a different role that is right for them—and for the company.

When designing a job rotation program, consider steps such as the request process, eligibility, matching participants to opportunities, the terms of rotation, timing, the transition plan, and monitoring the rotation.

Measuring the Success of the Program. With any new program, you will want to measure its success. Consider establishing key performance indicators (KPIs) that are tied to each of the program's goals and objectives. Some KPIs may be the number of rotations in a given year, the attrition rate, employee satisfaction, and the percentage of new skills learned.

Start Now, Don't Wait until the Economy Picks Up. If you believe that a job rotation program may help you attract, motivate, and retain your staff, now is the time to get started. It will not cost you anything other than time and effort.

The process alone will create a positive buzz in your department. Even if you retain one or two of your top employees each year, the program will pay for itself. I was recently watching a news segment on which the CEO of a major fast-food company was being interviewed about the past quarter performance, which had been markedly better than previous quarters. When asked by the reporter why business had picked up so dramatically, the CEO replied it was because the company started offering fat-free muffins and doughnuts. The reporter inquired, "So the fat-free items drove the sales?" "No," said the CEO. "The fat-free items aren't selling as well as expected, but it drove a lot of traffic into our stores because we gave customers a choice."

The point is that if you give people a choice, it makes them happier. By offering the fat-free items, the fast-food chain was perceived as a healthier franchise, and more customers visited the store—but bought the higher-fat items. Similarly, if you offer talent management programs, don't expect everyone to take advantage of the programs. Be assured that just by offering the programs, you have given people one more reason to stay with the company.

Retain Your Best Employees

While I have described several programs that touch on retaining your staff, I have decided to devote a section to describing some helpful strategies to make sure you hold on to your best and brightest employees. If you haven't figured it out by now, your human capital is your most important strategic asset.

Let's take a closer look at the issue. According to the Economist Intelligence Unit, a business information arm of the Economist Group, the publisher of the *Economist*, 30 percent of those surveyed believe that the levels of trust in their organization are very low or quite low and they expect to see resignations, compared with 42 percent who believe that the levels of trust are high or very high. As managers become increasingly aware of the fact that their most capable employees will head to new jobs, the race is on for companies to rebuild levels of trust and motivation among their staff or risk undergoing a difficult path to recovery postrecession.

Moreover, in some places, employee engagement appears to have hit a low point, particularly in the United States, where a report from the Conference Board found that job satisfaction is falling. Only 45 percent of the respondents to its survey in 2010 reported that they were satisfied with their jobs, down from 52.1 percent in 2005. Meanwhile, research from Right Management in 2010 indicated that many workers were not happy with their current jobs, with 60 percent saying they intended to leave to go elsewhere.[2]

Retaining employees is a tough job, but it's the most important job that you have. Here are some methods:

- **Positive teamwork.** Creating a positive work environment is an important factor in keeping employees happy and wanting to stay. It really doesn't matter how much they love their jobs; if they are not getting along with others in the workplace, they will simply move on. So try and staff projects with people across the department so they get to know one another better.
- **Career advancement.** As mentioned earlier, creating standard job descriptions helps employees to understand not only what is required of them in their current roles but also what is expected of them in their next positions. Setting clear expectations and creating opportunities for career growth helps people to stay longer with a company.
- **Make sure people know they fit into the big picture.** Employees become more satisfied when they understand how their contributions are making a positive difference for the company. So make sure you point that out at every opportunity, whether it be at staff meetings, at roundtables, or one-on-one. Make sure your employees know that their work is meaningful.

According to a report written by Robert Half Technology titled *Workplace Redefined: Shifting Generational Attitudes during Economic Change*, your top performers will be instrumental in helping your organization take advantage of improving business conditions. Here is what the report suggests you do to help retain your employees:

- **Improve salary and benefits.** Top performers who feel they have made concessions during the recession will expect to be rewarded for their loyalty and sacrifices.
- **Invest in employees.** Employees who feel their firm is committed to their professional growth will be less likely to seek out other opportunities. One-third of the workers surveyed plan to enhance their skill sets as a result of the recession.
- **Focus on growth.** Continually provide employees with new challenges and experiences that will prepare them for positions of

increasing responsibilities. Support and mentor them as they grow in their roles.

- **Re-recruit the top performers.** Give your best people compelling reasons to stay with you. Talk with them about their career aspirations and find out what more you can do to help them as they grow in their roles.
- **Keep the praise flowing.** Do not wait until a turnaround seems well under way to show appreciation to your staff for a job well done. Frequent encouragement and team-building activities will keep motivation levels high and increase employee engagement.[3]

As you can see from this list, there is no single activity that will keep a valued staff member from leaving the company. You will need to combine the strategies discussed in this section with others described throughout this chapter to create an effective talent retention program. What is important is that you make retention a normal course of business and don't wait for a key employee to resign to realize how important he or she is to the company.

Provide Mentoring

Mentoring programs provide employees with opportunities for growth in soft skills and professional development, thus helping the employees to further develop their full potential. In this section, I will share stories of how companies have put mentoring into practice to derive tangible benefits.

Jim Gerry, the vice president of North America IT at Hyatt Hotels Corporation, incorporates mentoring into his talent development strategy. He and his leadership team each mentor several employees within and outside the IT function. Jim says, "In additional to the typical benefits you realize from a mentoring program, such as providing personalized coaching to individuals, you also gain tremendous insight from individuals across the business on how well IT is performing."

The mentoring discussions also create an ecosystem of knowledge across the business that enables Jim's team to identify opportunities to rotate staff into new positions. Jim adds, "By mentoring employees outside your department, you get a lens on the top talent in the business—as well as potential job opportunities for your staff. That comes in handy when you need to fill a position or you have an employee who is interested in a rotation to a different department."

Mentoring programs provide employees with opportunities for growth in soft skills and professional development, thus helping the employees to further develop their full potential.

Terex CIO Fell offers an interesting twist on mentoring:

> *Over my career, I have discovered group mentoring to be more effective and productive than individualized mentoring. At Terex, I created mentoring circles, which is essentially a group of six or seven IT employees who meet on a regular basis. While an IT leader is responsible for facilitating the meetings, all members contribute to the discussions that vary between encouraging self-development, resolving business issues, improving operational excellence, and identifying opportunities to leverage technology to drive business results.*

I asked Brian R. Lurie, the senior vice president and CIO of Teleflex, about his view on mentoring. "Our mentoring program is customized for each of our high potentials [HIPOs]," he says. "A single mentor isn't assigned to a HIPO for life. A HIPO may have several mentors assigned to them, each one with a high level of proficiency in a particular skill that the HIPO needs to improve upon."

Retain Critical Skills

Since technology is threaded throughout most business processes these days, a company's ability to achieve its goals is increasingly dependent on the effectiveness of its IT strategies and professionals. IT leaders are expected to identify opportunities, adopt new technologies, and make the most cost-effective use of the latest technology while supporting legacy systems. The leaders are also expected to mitigate the risk of losing employees with critical skills by ensuring that others are experienced in those same skills as well.

Your IT staff has an inherent need to sustain the existing skills that keep your operations well supported. At the same time, being able to learn new skills to meet challenging business demands is equally important. Categorizing skills into levels of importance to the business helps to identify the most important skills as critical.

Critical skills assessment modeling (CSAM) is a best practice that helps IT leaders identify, assess, and retain critical skills for their business. By its very nature, CSAM helps you identify your HIPOs for both a management and a technical career track. By identifying the most critical skills in your department, including technical and people leadership skills, you can quantitatively identify your most valued employees.

I had the pleasure of working for Ken Harris, the CIO of Shaklee, when he was the CIO at Pepsi-Cola in the late 1990s. Ken introduced a very specific performance review process, which he refers to as the IT calibration process. He has used the process throughout his career, including at Nike, at the Gap, and now at Shaklee. His process is very much in line with the CSAM practice that I will explain shortly. Here's how Ken describes his IT calibration process:

> *Every year, I gather my people leaders in a room and have them rank the people below them on about ten core competencies, such as ability to deliver results, team player, technical skills, dealing with ambiguity, etc. The individuals are ranked on a scale of 1 to 5, where 5 is defined as a "role model." We use a bell curve so no more than 10 percent of the staff can be ranked as a role model with any particular competency. The process forces the raters to identify the top performers for each of the core competencies.*
>
> *I then ask the least senior people in the room to leave so the remaining members can rank them. You get two things out of the process: First, you get a clear assessment of your people. Second, your people come out of it knowing which behaviors are important to you. The process is extremely helpful when you start in a new role, but also something to repeat from time to time to get a fresh perspective on your staff.*

Critical skills assessment modeling (CSAM) is a best practice that helps IT leaders identify, assess, and retain critical skills for their business.

Critical Skills Assessment Modeling

Simply put, CSAM is a process whereby you identify the critical skills in your department as well as any gaps in experience and capacity with those skills. If you have gaps in either category, you and your company are at risk. The following outline is a simple, step-by-step guide to implementing a CSAM program for your business.

Step 1: Establish an Inventory of Critical Skills. Work with your staff to create a list of IT skills that are critical to support the business. After you have established the list, categorize the skills by functional area (e.g., desktop, networking, accounting applications, and system security). Identify the functional owners of each skill. For example, the skills relating to supporting an accounting system are typically owned by the IT manager of the accounting system or team.

Step 2: Have the Staff Members Assess Themselves. The next step is to work one-on-one with the staff members so they can rate themselves on their level of proficiency with each skill. Ideally, there should be a healthy mix of expertise as well as an opportunity to gain further knowledge. Several companies already ask their staff members to perform annual self-assessments on various competencies as part of a performance review. The difference with CSAM is it helps the departments get an understanding of the employees with experience in the critical skills and the amount of coverage available in the department.

Here is an example of a rating system:

Level 1. *Working knowledge* of the process and/or technology skill. The individual can provide limited support for the process and/or technology skill.

Level 2. *Proficient* in the process and/or technology skill. The individual can:
- Support the implementation of the process and/or technology skill.
- Support the delivery of training on the topic and assist with supporting users.
- Demonstrate experience with the process and/or system.
- Troubleshoot and resolve some issues.
- Assist with the authoring of technical specifications for changes that are moderate in complexity, including integration between systems.

Level 3. *Expert* in the process and/or technology skill. The individual can:

- Lead and execute the implementation of the process and/or technology.
- Deliver training on the topic to users.
- Troubleshoot and resolve the most complex issues.
- Independently author technical specifications for significant changes to the system, including integration between systems.

Step 3: Have the Managers Assess the Staff Members. After the staff members complete the self-assessment, the managers should assess them for the same skills identified above. This is common in the performance review process; implementing CSAM just adds another level of detail and dialogue relating to capabilities and performance. The fundamental difference is that CSAM helps you rate technical skills, not just soft skills.

If a skill is owned by another IT function, do not have the staff members rate themselves on the skill without consensus from the skill owner. I have observed situations where individuals rated themselves on skills from another IT function and the manager of the function did not agree that an individual had experience in the skill.

Step 4: Perform a Risk Analysis. Once you have conducted both assessments, you can determine your level of risk with each of the critical skills in your department. Here are examples of risks to examine:

High Risk
- Critical skills with no coverage.
- Critical skills with only one employee rated at any level (no backup).

Medium Risk
- Several employees have proficiency in a skill, but there are no experts.

Low Risk
- Only one expert, but several employees have proficiency with a skill.

Step 5: Build a Mitigation Plan. Once all critical skills have been identified and assessed, work with your management team to identify potential risks in their functional areas. After you have identified all of the risks, develop a mitigation plan, which should initially focus on creating activities to alleviate any high-risk areas. Mitigation plans can consist of actions on how to close gaps immediately or be more involved and include training, hiring consultants, or even outsourcing the skill. Each critical skill that is deemed a high risk should have a mitigation plan with a specific completion date. After you have established a plan for the high-risk skills, move on to create plans for medium-risk and low-risk skills.

The Challenges in Building CSAM

The fundamental purpose of CSAM is to ensure that your organization has adequate coverage for all critical skills despite the natural course of attrition. While it naturally helps you identify the strong as well as the weak players in your department, CSAM should be implemented with caution so as to avoid people panicking by assuming that you are using the information to reduce the staff. If your staff perceives that the purpose of the assessment is to weed out less-experienced employees, they will rate themselves higher on skills even though they may not possess the knowledge and experience of that level. If this happens, you will never get a realistic assessment of your team.

As IT leaders, you must communicate your vision clearly and maintain a collegial environment throughout the CSAM process. If you do this, your teams will have a positive view of the program and welcome the exercise as an opportunity for them to build skills and improve their ability to deliver value to the business.

Cultivate High Potential

High-potential employees (HIPOs) are your top performers: the 20 percent of employees who perform 80 percent of the work. HIPOs are passionate, have a very strong work ethic, and are typically characterized by quick promotions. As the future leaders of their organizations, HIPOs are often given assignments in different functions to stretch them and broaden their exposure to the business. They are expected to deliver superior performances.

Take the Show on the Road

Recently I had the pleasure of hearing Ramon Baez, the vice president and CIO of Kimberly-Clark Corporation, speak at the Fairfield-Westchester Society for Information Management CIO Executive Summit in Greenwich, Connecticut. Ramon spoke about several topics, including talent development and retention. At one point, he described a component of the development program for his HIPOs. Ramon referred to his first group of identified HIPOs as wave one and had them travel as a group to visit with executives at some of the top technology companies, including Microsoft, Apple, Google, SAP, Cisco, and Salesforce.com, among others. Since some of his deputies had never visited the companies, they joined the group on the visits.

> HIPOs are your top performers: the 20 percent of employees who perform 80 percent of the work.

During each visit, he had one of his HIPOs give a presentation on some of the IT initiatives going on at Kimberly-Clark. Upon returning from the visits, each of the members of the wave-one team was asked to mentor two other leaders in the organization, creating a pipeline of successors for the company.

Hyatt vice president Gerry has a tremendous passion for talent development. Here is how he and the leadership team are grooming talent at Hyatt:

> I report to the CFO, so we established a joint program to develop our IT and finance staff at Hyatt. The program consists of a top-down and bottom-up approach to talent management.
>
> From a top-down perspective, we instituted a finance IT leadership academy, which focuses on developing and retaining high potential employees [HIPOs]. The academy involves a series of activities around self-discovery

and exposure to senior leadership, including a 360-degree feedback process involving the participation of business and IT stakeholders. As part of the program, HIPOs get exposure to the Hyatt leadership team. We also retained the assistance of an outside coach to work with each of our HIPOs to help them fine-tune their skills in the 20–30 competencies that we measure.

From a bottom-up perspective, we use a traditional, albeit tactical, approach that has served us very well. We have a competency model that describes the skills and behaviors that are expected of each of the job roles, from software architect to business systems analyst. The expectations are set up front with our employees and measured by observing results over time. This performance management approach helps us determine whether an individual should be afforded a promotion or perhaps a rotation into a different role. While I realize our approach isn't new or groundbreaking, it was new to us up until just a few years ago and has paid off in terms of individual development.

What may be somewhat unique at Hyatt is we incorporate our talent management program into our five-year strategic planning process. The finance and IT leadership team meets twice a year to review individual progress toward development areas, identify additional HIPOs, evaluate promotion readiness, perform succession planning, and discuss opportunities for job rotations. The activity helps us to align our talent with our strategic plan and assure we have resources in place to achieve business goals and objectives.

For instance, if we are going to have a major transformation in the finance area that requires resources to be reallocated to the initiative, we discuss how to prepare individuals to backfill roles. In fact, IT has been a great net exporter of talent to business functions at Hyatt, which is a nice compliment for our development program.

The CIOs I talked to while performing research for this book all have a passion for helping their staffs succeed in their careers. Their strategies and techniques may be different, but their goals are the same. Shaklee CIO Harris says, "The thing I am most proud of is helping others grow in their careers. In fact, I keep a list of former employees who have attained CIO status; at last count, 16 people have earned CIO appointments. It is a personal objective of mine and one that I find extremely rewarding. I share the list with my staff so they know that I value their careers and that I am there for them."

Build a Management Development Program

A common method for nurturing your HIPOs is a management development program to prepare them for all aspects of current and anticipated responsibilities. This program is designed in part to fill in the gaps in the experiences of the managers as they seek to master their roles and prepare for broader responsibilities. The programs have synergies with the team-building programs described earlier, but they differ by helping up-and-coming executives expand their business acumen and by emphasizing the connection between management decisions and business results. They also typically involve coaching and mentoring components to maximize the effect the participants will have when they return to their jobs.

I asked Gary Boyd, the president of Operation Explore, to share some best practices in creating a management development program. Here is what he told me:

> We generally like to start with an assessment of the participants to gain an understanding of how well they know themselves, their teammates, and the business before entering a development process. The assessments come in a variety of methods, including a 360-degree feedback tool, where participants are evaluated by supervisors, peers, and direct reports along with the self-assessment 360.
>
> Other options for self-awareness psychometrics are personal, like the DiSC profile; or a team role preference, such as the Belbin Team Roles; or a personality assessment, like the Myers-Briggs Type Indicator.
>
> Another way to put actions into words is the integration of a competency model that allows for individual development planning based on the competencies specific to their jobs or company. This gives individuals a deep dive of psychometrics about themselves and the people around them.
>
> Once we have completed the assessment process, our goal is to develop these skills using the change process of (1) awareness, (2) understanding, (3) application, and finally (4) commitment. We use the assessments to create awareness that leads to understanding. Once we have built awareness and understanding, we create opportunities for application using action learning exercises where they can apply and hone their skills.

A specific example is the teaching and then application of a group problem-solving model learned in a classroom environment. Next we have smaller teams roll up their sleeves and apply the model to a novel experiential learning activity, where they typically revert back into their natural individual problem-solving behaviors as opposed to applying a new method or model for group problem solving.

Next we assign the team to work on an actual business initiative and solve a real issue that the company is facing. This allows individuals and teams to walk through the change process of awareness, understanding, application, and commitment. Using this process, participants are developing individual leadership and management skills while tackling real-world challenges.

Kevin Nash, the president of Aspen Organization Development Consulting, likes to anchor his programs on a variety of leadership development models:

There are many different leadership development models available such as situational leadership, servant leadership, transformational leadership, and integral leadership. To one degree or another, they all have some validity to them. The one that I favor is the integral leadership model, which involves helping people understand themselves with respect to their mind-sets, values, goals, capabilities, and situational dynamics. It also helps people to raise awareness of how their personal styles are perceived by others through normal interactions and what they can do to improve their performance.

Another model that I apply in my management development programs is called "leadership derailers." It is based on the work of Robert Hogan, who defines 11 personality traits that may derail leaders. Hogan's contention is that when people are under stress they revert to their comfort zones and exaggerate behaviors to protect themselves psychologically. The problem is that some of these behaviors can destroy their credibility.

For example, you may have a leader who is very confident and self-assured who becomes obnoxious and overbearing when under stress. The model helps an individual become more aware of their hot buttons and provides techniques to control the less desirable behaviors. A best practice is to integrate multiple leadership models into a management development program to help the participants get a variety of perspectives on their leadership style and identify a range of tools to help them improve.

Another View: Should You Single Out Your Stars?

According to a report released by the consulting firm Towers Watson, just 68 percent of companies formally identify HIPOs, and only 28 percent actually tell the employees they've been labeled as such. The survey was based on a study of 316 companies across North America.

There has been much debate on whether to tell HIPOs they are HIPOs. Some companies argue that a star system can be counterproductive. The reason is that singling out top performers can actually hasten their departure while alienating other people. "If you tell me I'm a high performer—one in ten—I'm going to tell that to a headhunter," says Mike Croxson of Synovus Financial. In this environment, singling out team members runs counter to fundamental precepts. As Croxson puts it, "You can't say, 'We're a high-potential company' and then look at two people and say, 'You're high potential, and you're low potential.' Folks on the team aren't stupid. They see the disconnect."[4]

Recruit the Best

In a down economy, companies receive hundreds of resumes for a single opening, making it difficult to identify qualified candidates. In 2011, Starbucks Corporation attracted 7.6 million job applicants for 65,000 corporate and retail openings. Procter & Gamble got nearly 1 million applications in the same time frame for 2,000 new or vacant positions.[5] Some companies are enlisting creative approaches to selecting the best candidates for their positions. Here is a summary of my findings:

- **Open house.** One option is inviting eligible candidates to a group event, such as an open house. This is a good way to expedite the process of interviewing a large pool of qualified people for your open positions.

  A consulting startup, I Love Rewards Inc., describes how, of the 1,200 applicants who were invited to the open house, only

400 actually came. The CEO told the *Wall Street Journal*, "That's self-selection. . . . It's so easy to apply for anything, but 800 didn't take the first step. That lowered the screening process." Interacting with potential candidates in a group setting is an excellent way to see their characters, levels of interest, working knowledge, and communication skills. It also lets you see if they're a good fit with your corporate culture.[6]

- **College recruiting in groups.** About 10 years ago, I worked for Boehringer-Ingelheim Inc., a large privately held pharmaceutical company. One of my first initiatives was to expand the staff by recruiting graduating college students. I worked with a team to visit top universities all around the country, where we interviewed hundreds of students. While I have participated in college recruiting many times over the course of my career, this was the first time I had done so with such a large volume. In a few months, we identified students to bring back for second interviews.

    However, instead of bringing the students back to our offices one by one, we decided to organize a group interview. We invited the qualifying candidates to our offices for a second round of interviews that took place over the course of several days. Since some of the students came from the same universities, we were able to save a few dollars in transportation costs. We were also able to get group-rate discounts at nearby hotels.

    We selected directors and managers to interview the candidates based on the skills they were interested in for their areas. A candidate who passed an interview with the first interviewer would be handed to the next interviewer. We used a predefined list of questions to avoid having interviewers ask the same questions over and over (although sometimes we purposely asked the same question multiple times to determine if we received the same answer each time).

    In a matter of days, we were able to narrow down the list of candidates to a few dozen potential hires. If we had decided to bring back the candidates individually, it would have taken weeks to accomplish the same objective, and it would have cost us more time and money.

- **Behavioral interviewing.** In "Behavioral Job Interviewing Strategies for Job-Seekers," Katharine Hansen describes the trend in behavioral interviewing:

> Traditional interviewing involves asking straight-forward questions such as "Tell me about a recent major achievement." The interviewer rarely follows up with more probing questions to learn how the candidate would handle himself in certain situations. Without more probing questions, it's very easy to tell the interviewer what they think they want to hear without allowing them to get a sense of the candidate's normal behavior.
>
> In a behavioral interview, however, it's much more difficult to give responses that are untrue to the candidate's character. When you start to tell a behavioral story, the behavioral interviewer typically will pick it apart to try to get at the specific behaviors. The interviewer will probe further for more depth or detail such as "What were you thinking at that point?" or "Tell me more about your meeting with that person," or "Lead me through your decision process." If the candidate told a story that's anything but totally honest, his response will not hold up through the barrage of probing questions.
>
> Employers use the behavioral interview technique to evaluate a candidate's experiences and behaviors so they can determine the applicant's potential for success. The interviewer identifies job-related experiences, behaviors, knowledge, skills, and abilities that the company has decided are desirable in a particular position. For example, some of the characteristics that companies look for include:
>
> - Critical thinking
> - Being a self-starter
> - Willingness to learn
> - Willingness to travel
> - Self-confidence
> - Teamwork
> - Professionalism
>
> The employer then structures very pointed questions to elicit detailed responses aimed at determining if the candidate possesses the desired characteristics. Questions (often not even framed as a question) typically start out: "Tell about a time . . . " or "Describe a situation . . . "

Many employers use a rating system to evaluate selected criteria during the interview.[7]

Kevin Nash, the president of Aspen Organization Development Consulting, doesn't believe that hiring should be straight from the gut:

> So many managers base their hiring decisions on intuition versus facts even though it's been shown, through numerous studies, that gut-based recruiting is not a reliable predictor of a successful hire. Conversely, gathering more data in the form of formal assessments can greatly increase your chances of recruiting the right candidate. The first step is to establish the critical success factors for a particular position. For instance, the critical success factors for a CFO are quite different from the head-of-sales position. In order to effectively recruit candidates for either of those roles, you need to understand the factors that lead to success.
>
> Next, run the candidates through personality assessments, problem-solving assessments, and a determination of cultural fit. These assessments are designed to determine their suitability for the position. We use this evidence-based approach with our clients, and they have found it to be an invaluable part of their recruitment efforts—they no longer recruit senior executives purely on gut instinct.

- **Abstract interviewing.** Some argue that traditional job interview questions are not very instrumental in helping firms hire the best candidates. There have been many studies on this topic, and most results demonstrate that interviewers make a hiring decision within the first few minutes of an interview. Not much has changed over the years, but the fact that there are so many candidates for each job opening has caused firms to search for something new. There is a growing trend for firms to use abstract questions and puzzles as part of the interview process.

  You may be thinking that this is the same as the traditional aptitude testing that has been going on for years, but you would be wrong. The new line of questioning is very different. In a composite of a Google interview, recently reported in a *Wall Street Journal* article written by William Poundstone, one of the questions a candidate was asked was "You are shrunk to the height of a nickel and thrown into a blender. Your mass is reduced so that your density is the same as usual. The blades start moving in 60 seconds. What do you do?"[8] As strange as the abstract questions may become, they do give the interviewer an opportunity to determine how well the candidate will fit into the company's culture.

Executive recruiters are an invaluable source of expertise on IT leadership, since they spend their days advising companies and help to recruit new executives. Over the course of my career, I have been fortunate to build a network of some of the top executive recruiters in the IT industry. I am truly grateful that they spent time sharing their insights with me on a variety of topics. Their words of wisdom are interspersed throughout this book.

I asked Phil Schneidermeyer, a partner at Heidrick & Struggles, to describe the qualities that CIOs look for when recruiting their direct reports. Here is what he told me:

> *First, you have to understand your leadership style and the culture of your organization. The better your understanding of these factors, the more success you will have in recruiting talent that can help you drive business outcomes. No one wants someone who is going to be disruptive. It shouldn't be surprising that many of the same qualities required to be a CIO also apply to their direct reports. For instance, most CIOs want their lieutenants to be able to develop strong relationships, effectively communicate, and speak in business terms. When they enter a room, they should be someone people want to listen to.*

Rich Brennen, a partner at Spencer Stuart, has a similar take on it:

> *Your direct reports have to fit your company's culture. You can't afford to have people who are going to work against the grain of company. Your direct reports interface directly with your most important IT clients, and it is critical that they are in step with the business. Also, they need to come with a great deal of business acumen—particularly as IT morphs into more of an assembler of technology rather than a creator of technology. Finally, they need to be a positive ambassador for you and the IT organization. IT is most visible to the business when it fails than when it succeeds. And when it fails, you want to have people your business stakeholders like and respect.*

Foster Teamwork through Community Service

A great way to unite your team, build leadership skills, and serve the community at the same time is to have a community service event. It's a great alternative to a traditional team-building program.

You can include your staff, your peers and their staff, and even technology providers. The event can help you address multiple talent management objectives such as strengthening morale, developing project leadership skills, and fostering relationships—all while helping the community. I have participated and even led many of these types of events over the years, and they have always exceeded my expectations in terms of benefits.

> People often walk away from a volunteering activity feeling fulfilled and having a sense of pride in themselves and their teammates.

One of the most significant benefits people get from volunteering is incorporating service into their lives and making a difference in the community. I have heard people say that with community service, some of the benefits are what you *see*, while other benefits are what you *feel*. People often walk away from a volunteering activity feeling fulfilled and having a sense of pride in themselves and their teammates. If you can incorporate volunteering into a team-building activity, you will help connect with your team *and* have them gain a sense of community.

Recognize and Reward Employees

It's no surprise that great talent is the only sustainable strategic advantage. And yet retaining it still eludes many organizations. Let's examine some of the best practices to providing informal recognition to your top talent.

It doesn't cost much to recognize an employee for a doing a good job, yet we often miss the opportunity. A little recognition goes a long way in terms of motivation and loyalty. Here are some ways to informally acknowledge employee performance:

- **Use good timing.** Timing is very important. The sooner you thank someone for doing something special, the more of a positive impact it will have on the person.
- **Use gestures of appreciation.** Praise can be as simple as thanking an individual or team in person, making a phone call, giving a handwritten card, or even sending a short e-mail. The more personable the delivery, the greater the impact; the important thing is to just do it.

- **Make recognition contingent.** Recognition is most powerful when it's contingent on performance and not some generic gesture of acknowledgment to a group. Companies will bring in doughnuts on Friday and give people cards on their birthday, and all of a sudden they have an entitlement culture. If you do stuff just to be nice, people end up expecting more. So make recognition contingent on desired behavior and performance; your employees will value the recognition more, and you'll get better results. You also need to keep it fresh, relevant, and sincere. Any incentive has less punch with repeated use.[9]

- **Be supportive and involved.** According to a survey, the top factor that people valued in terms of recognition was "managerial support and involvement": asking employees their opinions, involving them in decisions, giving them authority to do their jobs, supporting them when they made a mistake, and so forth. Employees want basic praise. In the top 10 factors, there were 4 types of praise: personal praise, written praise, public praise, and electronic praise. Those are the hottest ones for people, and none of them cost a dime.[10]

- **Make a Wall of Fame.** One of my favorite recognition methods is forwarding and posting complimentary e-mails from business partners praising one of my staff members or teams. I forward these e-mails to my entire staff and then print and hang on our Wall of Fame, which is essentially a billboard located in a well-traveled corridor. This type of recognition achieves two objectives: First, it makes the individual recognized by the business partner feel great. Second, it communicates and encourages the desired behavior to the rest of my team.

- **Give awards.** Consider creating an annual awards program. You can create different types of awards to cover each of your functional areas. For instance, you can have an innovation award for business software and a separate innovation award for a pure infrastructure project. It helps to have your staff and business partners vote to determine the winners rather than leaving it to the IT leadership team to select the winners. Other award categories can be user satisfaction results, help desk ticket performance, and so on.

It doesn't cost much to recognize an employee for a doing a good job, yet we often miss the opportunity. A little recognition goes a long way in terms of motivation and loyalty.

Build Your Personal Brand

According to Marc J. Schiller, author of *The 11 Secrets of Highly Influential IT Leaders*, in order for you to maximize your influence and respect at your home business, you need to establish a respected presence away from home. Here is what he wrote:

> To be held in high regard within your company you need to be held in high regard outside your company. Practically, this means that you need to establish a reputation for yourself and your team outside the walls of your own company. You and your team need to be seen on the playing field of your industry and beyond.[11]

The recognition can be in the form of industry awards, invitations to speak at conferences, interviews with trade journals, and so forth. You are a product of your own invention. You need to consider yourself as a product or a brand and market yourself internally and externally. When you build an awareness of your capabilities, doors begin to open for you. You get invited to be on governance boards for major conferences or even participate on public and private company boards.

Prepare Yourself for the New Workforce

As I end this chapter on talent management, I think it would be interesting to examine how some of the major trends in technology are affecting our future workforce. Schneidermeyer of Heidrick & Struggles believes that CIOs should lead the discussion on how companies should embrace consumerization to better prepare for the new workforce:

> *With the advent of cloud computing, social media, and mobilization, we are at the front end of experiencing a dramatic shift in business as millennials join our workforce and change the way we work. Millennials are accustomed to using their own technology, working in teams, and being connected all*

of the time. If you are going to be a transformational CIO, you have to understand and embrace the consumerization of technology and learn to apply it to your business.

Top Plays

- Job descriptions serve as the basis for all other talent acquisition and development strategies.
- IT training is usually the first thing to get cut and the last thing to come back. Don't make this mistake.
- CSAM helps you identify critical skills in your department and any gaps in experience and capacity with those skills.
- High-potential employees, or HIPOs, are your top performers— the 20 percent of employees who perform 80 percent of the work.
- Enlist creative approaches to selecting the best candidates for your open positions.
- A great way to unite your team, build leadership skills, and serve the community at the same time is to have a community service event.
- A little recognition goes a long way in terms of motivation and loyalty.
- You are a product of your own invention. You need to consider yourself as a product or a brand and market yourself internally and externally.

Notes

1. Ladan Nikravan, "Back to Class," *Chief Learning Officer*, January 2012.
2. Economist Intelligence Unit, *Companies at a Crossroads* (Luton, UK: Lumesse, 2010).
3. Robert Half Technology, *Workplace Redefined: Shifting Generational Attitudes during Economic Change* (Menlo Park, CA: privately printed, 2010), 1–16.
4. *Retaining Your Best People: The Results Driven Manager* (Boston: Harvard Business School Press, 2006).

5. Lauren Weber, "Your Resume vs. Oblivion," *Wall Street Journal*, January 24, 2012.

6. Bianca Male, "10 Creative Recruiting Strategies to Hire Great People," *Business Insider*, February 25, 2010, http://www.businessinsider.com/10-creative-recruiting-strategies-for-finding-great-hires-2010-2# (accessed December 27, 2011).

7. Katharine, Hansen, "Behavioral Job Interviewing Strategies for Job-Seekers," Quintessential Careers, http://www.quintcareers.com/behavioral_interviewing.html (accessed December 27, 2011).

8. William Poundstone, "How to Ace a Google Interview," *Wall Street Journal*, December 24–25, 2011.

9. *Retaining Your Best People*, 105.

10. *Ibid.*, 106.

11. Marc J. Schiller, *The 11 Secrets of Highly Influential IT Leaders* (Mamaroneck, NY: privately printed, 2011), 133.

Conclusion

The price of success is hard work, dedication to the job at hand, and the determination that whether we win or lose, we have applied the best of ourselves to the task at hand.

—Vince Lombardi

Touchdown Passes

We all have certain strategies that we develop over the course of our careers and apply when the applicable situation presents itself. In football, the term *touchdown pass* is the most prestigious statistic among quarterbacks. So in the spirit of the name of this book, I decided to dedicate the Conclusion to sharing my touchdown passes, which are essentially strategies that have earned me points throughout my career. As a leader, you need a team, and just as in football, you need someone to pass to in order to score points. The passes described here are not in any particular order, and some have already been mentioned earlier in this book, but they are worth reiterating because of how often I tend to use them. I hope you find them as useful in your current role and throughout your career as I have.

Use Governance to Avoid Chaos

In Chapter 3, I described how to build a governance framework to ensure the linkage of business and IT plans; to define, maintain, and validate the IT value proposition; and to partner with enterprise operations. Governance is one of my touchdown passes because without it you basically have chaos: whoever screams the loudest will get your attention. Without governance, important initiatives will be derailed by the constant changes in priorities. Within 90 days of starting a new job, you should be well on your way to forming a governance framework for your department. Governance is how work gets done—period.

Show People How They Fit In

The strategic planning process helps you to create and communicate your vision and allows people to understand their purpose in the organization. Make sure your staff is aligned with the vision, mission, goals, and objectives of the department. People want to understand how they fit into the big picture. So start by creating departmental goals and cascading those goals to every member in your department. After you cascade your goals to your direct reports, they should add their specific objectives, designed to meet your goals, and cascade them to their staff. At the end of the exercise, everyone in the department will have a set of goals and objectives that are aligned with the department's vision. By performing this exercise, everyone will understand how they are contributing to the success of the department.

Just Say No

It is important to say no to distractions because doing so will keep you focused on the game. Once you have worked with your business partners to define your strategies and objectives for the year, you need to relentlessly scrutinize every attempt—and there will be attempts—to distract you from getting those touchdowns. This is not to say that you shouldn't be agile and not be able to adapt to new business demands. It means it's your job to rigorously challenge new demands to make

Conclusion 201

sure they are worth distracting you and your team from previously agreed-on objectives. If you say yes to every demand, I can guarantee you nothing will ever get done.

Don't Be Afraid to Take Risks

I am always hoping to succeed, but I am not afraid to fail. I just don't want to land in between. You come to make better decisions by making not-so-good decisions and then correcting them. You get to become a good IT leader by creating a vision, influencing others to follow you, and seeing the results over and over. You may not get it right the first time around, but practice makes perfect. As the old joke has it, the answer to the tourist's question "How do I get to Carnegie Hall?" is "Practice, practice, practice."

Manage Operational Performance

Just as a president of a division or a COO reviews many operational reports to monitor and manage the business, a CIO needs to consider similar practices to effectively run his or her shop. In Chapter 5, I described the key reports that CIOs should have to manage their operations.

When you have meetings with your staff, you should be reviewing the information in the reports that I described. You should get to a point where your staff can rattle off the metrics as well as you can. When that day comes, you will know that people understand how the department is being measured and what they need to focus on to continuously improve operations.

Use Meetings to Drive Deliverables

Most of us absolutely dread going to meetings. They are usually a big waste of time because the facilitator doesn't have a clue about what he or she is trying to achieve. There is usually a lack of any sort of agenda, or if there is one it's usually a couple of bullet points hastily thrown together right before the meeting. You are usually lucky to get any materials to review ahead of time. In fact, one of my pet peeves is attending a meeting where the facilitator hands out a stack of papers to read during the meeting. Yeah, like that's actually going to happen. If you don't get materials to me ahead of the meeting, there is zero chance I'm going to begin reading the materials at the meeting. *Meetings are for discussing, not reading.* Reading should be done ahead of time so that you can ask questions or form opinions based on the information. I'm also a "one-pager"; I think most issues and proposals can be summarized on a single page. But I still want the one page *before* the meeting!

So why did I title this touchdown play "Use Meetings to Drive Deliverables" if I obviously don't care much for meetings? It's not that I don't think meetings are useful, I just don't think some people know how to run them effectively.

I do, in fact, believe meetings can be tremendously useful in getting people to deliver on their promises. People are busy—they get one deadline after another, so it's not surprising they occasionally miss deadlines. I'm just not very happy when they miss one of mine. Want to know how to ensure someone doesn't miss a deadline? Schedule a meeting the day of the deadline! Missing a meeting is not culturally acceptable in most organizations, and who wants to come to class without their homework being complete?

That's right—if someone needs to define the business requirements for a major project, schedule a meeting to review the requirements the day of the deadline. Of course, you only need to do this one time after someone misses a deadline; it usually won't happen again.

Build Awesome Teams

Let's face it; a leader isn't anything without having people to follow him or her—and people are stronger when they work as part of a team. As Patrick Lencioni wrote in his highly popularized book, *The Five Dysfunctions of a Team*, "Not finance. Not strategy. Not technology. It is teamwork that remains the ultimate competitive advantage, both because it is so powerful and so rare."[1]

In Chapter 7, I described the talent management strategies that I have personally used over the course of my career. I wrote about them because I know from personal experience that they work, and I wanted to help others be successful with building their teams. It's not easy to build an awesome team, but you can't sit back and hope that it will happen by itself—you have to work for it.

Notes

1. Patrick Lencioni, *The Five Dysfunctions of a Team* (San Francisco: Jossey-Bass, 2002), vii.

Bibliography

Items that are asterisked are also recommended for further reading.

Accenture. *Beyond Centralization: Driving High Performance through Fully Realized Shared Services*. Chicago: privately printed, 2007.

Adelsberg, David van, and Edward A. Trolley. *Running Training Like a Business: Delivering Unmistakable Value*. San Francisco: Berrett-Koehler, 1999.

Alessandra, Tony, and Phillip L. Hunsaker. *Presentation Power*. Carlsbad, CA: privately printed, 2005.

Barrow, Greg. "5 Benefits of a Social Media Risk Management Program." *Social Media Today*, February 17, 2011. http://socialmediatoday.com/gregbarrow/271023/5-benefits-social-media-risk-management-program.

★Bates, Suzanne. *Motivate Like a CEO: Communicate Your Strategic Vision and Inspire People to Act!* New York: McGraw-Hill, 2009.

Binder, Jean. *Global Project Management: Communication, Collaboration and Management across Borders*. Farnham, UK: Gower, 2007.

Bjorlin, Courtney. "How to Build an SAP Super User Program That Will Last." *ASUG News*, July 1, 2011.

Borgman, Christine L. *From Gutenberg to the Global Information Infrastructure: Access to Information in the Networked World*. London: MIT Press, 2003.

Brainin, Esther. "Experiences of Cultures in Global ERP Implementation." Enterprise Resource Planning for Global Economies: Managerial Issues and

Challenges. *IGI Global*, 2008: 167–188. March 27, 2012. doi:10.4018/978-1-59904-531-3.ch010

★Bridges, William. *Managing Transitions: Making the Most of Change*, 2nd ed. Cambridge, MA: privately printed, 2003.

Brodkin, Jon. "Gartner: Seven Cloud-Computing Security Risks." *InfoWorld*, July 2, 2008.

Carr, Nicholas. "IT Doesn't Matter." *Harvard Business Review*, May 1, 2003, 41–49.

Cloud Security Alliance. "Top Threats to Cloud Computing 1.0" White paper, March 2010. https://cloudsecurityalliance.org/topthreats/csathreats.v1.0.pdf.

Creswick, Brian P. *Developing Successful Organizational IT Strategies: IT Chargeback as a Component of Effective IT Financial Management*. McLean, VA: Project Performance, 2004.

Cringely, Robert. *Triumph of the Nerds: How the Personal Computer Changed the World*. (DVD). PBS, 1996.

CTIA Association. "CTIA's Survey Finds More Wireless Devices Than Americans." *CTIA SmartBrief*, October 11, 2011. http://www.smartbrief.com/news/ctia/associationNews.jsp (accessed October 17, 2011).

Dail, Baljit, and Andrew S. West. "Building Stronger IT Vendor Relationships." *McKinsey & Company Newsletter* (NJ), 2005.

Doran, G. T. "There's a S.M.A.R.T. Way to Write Management's Goals and Objectives." *Management Review*, 70(11): 1981, 35–36.

Economist Intelligence Unit. *Companies at a Crossroads*. Luton, UK: Lumesse, 2010.

Elings, Peter and Oliver, Doug. *Global Transformation Readiness*. CIO Insight. Deloitte Development, September 9, 2010. http://www.cioinsight.com/c/a/Globalization/Global-Transformation-Readiness-Part-4-432778.

Elky, Steve. "An Introduction to Information System Risk." SANS Institute InfoSec, May 31, 2006.

Gerritsen, Eric J. "The Global Infrastructure Boom of 2009–2015." *Journal of Commerce*, May 19, 2009. http://www.joc.com/commentary/white-paper-global-infrastructure-boom-2009-2015.

Hamel, Gary. *Leading the Revolution: How to Thrive in Turbulent Times by Making Innovation a Way of Life*. Boston: Harvard Business School Press, 2000.

Hansen, Katharine. "Behavioral Job Interviewing Strategies for Job-Seekers." *Quintessential Careers*. http://www.quintcareers.com/behavioral_interviewing.html.

Hardy, Quentin. "More Wireless Devices Than People." *New York Times*, October 12, 2011.

Hawking, Paul. "Implementing ERP Systems Globally: A Case Study." *International Journal of Strategic Information Technology and Applications*, 1(3): 2010, 26–35.

*High, Peter A. *World Class IT: Why Businesses Succeed When IT Triumphs.* San Francisco: Jossey-Bass, 2009.

*Isaacson, Walter. *Steve Jobs.* New York: Simon & Schuster, 2011.

"IT Governance Framework." *Forrester Best Practice*, March 2005.

James, Geoffrey. "14 Easy Ways to Get Insanely Motivated." *Inc.*, December 19, 2011.

Jrliem. "New Skills Required for Cloud Computing Success." Cloud Computing, September 16, 2011. http://cloudcomputingx.org/new-skills-for-cloud-computing-success.html (accessed January 2, 2012).

*Kaplan, Robert S., and David P. Norton. *Strategy Maps: Converting Intangible Assets into Tangible Outcomes.* Boston: Harvard Business School Publishing, 2004.

Kepes, Ben. *Cloud U—Revolution Not Evolution: How Cloud Computing Differs from Traditional IT and Why It Matters.* Christchurch, NZ: Diversity, 2010.

King, Julia. "Chief of the Year," *CIO*, December 12, 2011.

———. "When IT Gets to Play: Skunk Works Projects Deliver Value." *ComputerWorld*, December 5, 2011.

Lencioni, Patrick. *The Five Dysfunctions of a Team.* San Francisco: Jossey-Bass, 2002.

Male, Bianca. "10 Creative Recruiting Strategies for Finding Great Hires," *Business Insider*, February 25, 2010. http://www.businessinsider.com/10-creative-recruiting-strategies-for-finding-great-hires-2010-2# (accessed December 27, 2011).

Nash, Kim S. "CIOs Forge Vendor Collectives to Extract Business Benefits." *CIO*, November 28, 2011.

Nikravan, Ladan. "Back to Class." *Chief Learning Officer*, January 2012.

Oracle. *Choosing the Number of Instances for JD Edwards EnterpriseOne.* Redwood Shores, CA: privately printed, 2007.

Oracle. *Positioning the CIO as a Powerful Business Partner with IT Portfolio Governance.* Redwood Shores, CA: privately printed, 2010.

Plummer, Daryl C., and Peter Middleton. *Predicts 2012: Four Forces Combine to Transform the IT Landscape,* December 9, 2011. http://www.gartner.com/id=1871420 (accessed January 5, 2012).

Posey, Brien. "IT Cloud Survival Skills." *Redmond*, May 1, 2010.

Poundstone, William. "How to Ace a Google Interview." *Wall Street Journal*, December 24–25, 2011.

Preston, Rob. "Top 10 CIO Priorities—and Perspective from India." *Information-Week*, October 31, 2011.

Rackham, Neil, Lawrence Friedman, and Richard Ruff. *Getting Partnering Right*. New York: McGraw-Hill, 1996.

Reed, John. "How to Find the Best Person for the Job." Robert Half Technology, June 23, 2011. http://www.cioupdate.com/career/article.php/3936351/How-to-Find-the-Best-Person-for-the-Job.htm (accessed January 2, 2012).

★*Retaining Your Best People: The Results Driven Manager*. Boston: Harvard Business School Press, 2006.

Riverbed Technology. *The CIO's New Guide to Design of Global IT Infrastructure*. San Francisco: privately printed, 2011.

Robert Half Technology. *Workplace Redefined: Shifting Generational Attitudes during Economic Change*. Menlo Park, CA: privately printed, 2010.

Roberts, Dan. *Unleashing the Power of IT: Bringing People, Business, and Technology Together*. Hoboken, NJ: John Wiley & Sons, 2011.

Salant, Priscilla, and Don A. Dillman. *How to Conduct Your Own Survey*. New York: John Wiley & Sons, 1994.

★Schiller, Marc J. *The 11 Secrets of Highly Influential IT Leaders*. Mamaroneck, NY: privately printed, 2011.

"Seven Tips on Keeping Your Mobile Devices Secure: Report on Smartphone Malware." *TechJournal*, June 9, 2011.

Shang, Shari, and Peter B. Seddon. "Assessing and Managing the Benefits of Enterprise Systems: The Business Manager's Perspective." *Blackwell Science Information Systems Journal*, 2002: 271–99.

Skarzynski, Peter, and Rowan Gibson. *Innovation to the Core: A Blueprint for Transforming the Way Your Company Innovates*. Boston: Harvard Business School Press, 2008.

Stoneburner, Gary, Alice Goguen, and Alexis Feringa. *Risk Management Guide for Information Technology Systems*. Gaithersburg, MD: National Institute of Standards and Technology, 2002.

Tantow, Martin. "5 Major Trends in Mobile Cloud Computing." *Cloud Times*, June 5, 2011. http://cloudtimes.org/5-major-trends-in-mobile-cloud-computing/ (accessed October 18, 2011).

Technology Group International. *Preparing a Request for Proposal (RFP)*. Toledo, OH: privately printed, 2009.

TIBCO Software. *TIBCO Service-Oriented IT Organizational Structure Best Practices: An Introduction*. Palo Alto, CA: privately printed, 2005.

"2010 State of the CIO Survey." *CIO*, January 2010

"2012 State of the CIO Survey." *CIO*, January 2012.

*VanGundy, Arthur B. *Getting to Innovation: Asking the Right Questions Generates the Great Ideas Your Company Needs.* New York: Amacom, 2007.

Wailgum, Thomas. "SMB ERP Projects: Don't Forget the ROI." *CIO*, April 1, 2009. http://www.cio.com/article/487794/SMB_ERP_Projects_Don_t_Forget_the_ROI (accessed November 5, 2010).

Weber, Lauren. "Your Resume vs. Oblivion." *Wall Street Journal*, January 24, 2012.

*Weill, Peter, and Jeanne W. Ross. *IT Governance: How Top Performers Manage IT Decision Rights for Superior Results.* Boston: Harvard Business School Publishing, 2004.

About the Author

Nicholas Colisto is a senior IT executive with over 26 years of experience delivering innovative technology-enabled business solutions in the consumer products, pharmaceutical, software, and construction industries. Throughout his career, he has led large transformational initiatives using technology to drive business value. Colisto serves as the vice president and chief information officer at Hovnanian Enterprises Inc., a large national homebuilder.

Prior to joining Hovnanian, he held IT leadership positions at global organizations including Pepsi-Cola, Priceline.com, Hyperion Solutions, Boehringer-Ingelheim, and Bayer Corporation.

Colisto is very active in the education, IT, and health-care communities. He lectures at Columbia University's CIO Institute. He serves on the academic advisory boards at Rutgers University and Brookdale Community College. He taught as an adjunct professor in IT at Manhattanville College in New York at the graduate level for several years and also served on the school's advisory board.

He is a member of the governing body for Evanta's CIO executive summits in New York and New Jersey and is a regular speaker. Colisto is a repeat guest on CIO talk radio, where he shares best practices on IT leadership and innovation. He is a member of the Society for Information Management (SIM) and serves on its governing body for CIO leadership summits.

Colisto also serves on the foundation board of trustees for Bayshore Community Hospital, part of the Meridian Health Network.

He is the recipient of seven industry awards, including the 2011 Computerworld Premier 100 IT Leaders, 2010 CIO 100 by IDG's *CIO* magazine, 2011 InformationWeek 100, 2011 InfoWorld Green 15, 2010 InformationWeek 500, 2009 InformationWeek 250, and 2009 InfoWorld 100.

Colisto holds a B.B.A. in management information systems and an M.S. in information systems from Pace University in New York.

He lives with his wife and two children in Marlboro, New Jersey.

About the Website

This book includes a companion website, which can be found at http://www.wiley.com/go/cioplaybook. The password to enter this site is Colisto.

The website features templates that were developed for each of the seven steps described in this book. They are straightforward and easily customizable by you or your staff to create similar documents for your own organization. The following templates are included:

- **Strategic Plan.** The purpose of this template is to describe the plan to direct and manage all IT resources in line with your company's business strategy and priorities.
- **Governance Framework.** The purpose of this template is to describe the guiding principles and procedures for managing the innovation for business software and supporting technologies.
- **Business Case.** This template will help you describe how your proposal will address current business concerns, the recommendations and rationale of the project, and the justification.
- **IT Scorecard.** Use this template to convey how IT is committed to delivering value by providing innovative, cost-effective products and services to your company.

- **Standard Responses to User Inquiries.** Save time and gain consistency by using this template, which includes seven sample letters to help you and your team members respond to questions and requests from your user audience.
- **System Feature Change Request.** Use this template to document and communicate a request for a new system feature or a change to an existing system feature.
- **Service Level Agreement.** This template is for users to describe the contract between the IT department and its users that specifies, in measurable terms, the services the IT department will furnish as well as the expectations and obligations of the user organization.
- **Critical Skills Assessment Model.** Use this template to assess the level of proficiency that your IT staff has with critical skills and determine if there are any gaps that require attention.
- **Job Rotation Program.** This template will help you document a program to systematically move employees from job to job within the department, as a method to attract, retain, and keep top talent on the cutting edge of knowledge, driving significant improvements in the ability of your department to perform.
- **IT Benchmarking.** This template will help you create a custom IT benchmarking survey for your company.

Index